GRAPHIC ORGANIZERS
AND OTHER
VISUAL STRATEGIES

ENGAGE THE
BRAIN

MARCIA L. TATE

CORWIN PRESS
Classroom

For information:

Corwin Press
A SAGE Publications Company
2455 Teller Road
Thousand Oaks, California 91320
CorwinPress.com

SAGE Publications, Ltd.
1 Oliver's Yard
55 City Road
London EC1Y 1SP
United Kingdom

SAGE Publications India Pvt. Ltd.
B 1/I 1 Mohan Cooperative
Industrial Area
Mathura Road, New Delhi
India 110 044

SAGE Publications Asia-Pacific Pvt. Ltd.
33 Pekin Street #02-01
Far East Square
Singapore 048763

Printed in the United States of America.

ISBN 978-1-4129-5230-9

This book is printed on acid-free paper.

08 09 10 11 12 10 9 8 7 6 5 4 3 2 1

Executive Editor: Kathleen Hex
Managing Developmental Editor: Christine Hood
Editorial Assistant: Anne O'Dell
Developmental Writer: Q. L. Pearce
Developmental Editor: Christine Hood
Proofreader: Bette Darwin
Art Director: Anthony D. Paular
Cover Designer: Monique Hahn
Interior Production Artist: Karine Hovsepian
Illustrator: Patrick Giourard
Design Consultant: PUMPKiN PIE Design

GRADES **6-8**

LANGUAGE ARTS

ENGAGE THE BRAIN

TABLE OF CONTENTS

Connections to Standards

This chart shows the national language arts standards that are covered in each chapter.

LANGUAGE ARTS	Standards are covered on pages
Read a wide range of print and nonprint texts to build an understanding of texts, of self, and of the cultures of the United States and the world; to acquire new information; to respond to the needs and demands of society and the workplace; and for personal fulfillment (includes fiction and nonfiction, classic, and contemporary works).	6, 19, 22, 28
Read a wide range of literature from many periods in many genres to build an understanding of the many dimensions (e.g., philosophical, ethical, aesthetic) of human experience.	9, 19, 22, 25, 28, 78,
Apply a wide range of strategies to comprehend, interpret, evaluate, and appreciate texts. Draw on prior experience, interactions with other readers and writers, knowledge of word meaning and of other texts, word identification strategies, and understanding of textual features (e.g., sound-letter correspondence, sentence structure, context, graphics).	9, 13, 16, 19, 22, 25, 35, 38, 41, 78
Adjust the use of spoken, written, and visual language (e.g., conventions, style, vocabulary) to communicate effectively with a variety of audiences and for different purposes.	13, 35, 44, 47, 54, 58, 65, 68, 75, 86, 93
Employ a wide range of strategies while writing, and use different writing process elements appropriately to communicate with different audiences for a variety of purposes.	35, 38, 47, 50, 54, 58, 62, 72, 75, 86, 93
Apply knowledge of language structure, language conventions (e.g., spelling and punctuation), media techniques, figurative language, and genre to create, critique, and discuss print and nonprint texts.	13, 41, 44, 58, 62, 65, 68, 72, 75, 82
Conduct research on issues and interests by generating ideas and questions, and by posing problems. Gather, evaluate, and synthesize data from a variety of sources (e.g., print and nonprint texts, artifacts, people) to communicate discoveries in ways that suit the purpose and audience.	16, 50, 89
Use a variety of technological and informational resources (e.g., libraries, databases, computer networks, video) to gather and synthesize information and to create and communicate knowledge.	16, 28, 41, 58, 72, 82, 89
Participate as knowledgeable, reflective, creative, and critical members of a variety of literacy communities.	41, 47, 50, 54, 82
Use spoken, written, and visual language to accomplish a purpose (e.g., for learning, enjoyment, persuasion, and the exchange of information).	9, 25, 35, 38, 41, 50, 54, 62, 65, 68, 75, 78, 86, 93

Introduction

An ancient Chinese proverb claims: "Tell me, I forget. Show me, I remember. Involve me, I understand." This timeless saying insinuates what all educators should know: Unless students are involved and actively engaged in learning, true learning rarely occurs.

The latest brain research reveals that both the right and left hemispheres of the brain should be engaged in the learning process. This is important because the hemispheres talk to one another over the corpus callosum, the structure that connects them. No strategies are better designed for this purpose than graphic organizers and visuals. Both of these strategies engage students' visual modality. More information goes into the brain visually than through any other modality. Therefore, it makes sense to take advantage of students' visual strengths to reinforce and make sense of learning.

How to Use This Book

Correlated with the national standards for language arts, the activities in this book are designed using strategies that actively engage the brain. They are presented in the way the brain learns best, to make sure students get the most out of each lesson: focus activity, modeling, guided practice, check for understanding, independent practice, and closing. Go through each step to ensure that students will be fully engaged in the concept being taught and understand its purpose and meaning.

Each step-by-step activity provides one or more visual tools students can use to make important connections between related concepts, structure their thinking, organize ideas logically, and reinforce learning. Graphic organizers and visuals include: Venn diagram, character pyramid, fishbone map, problem/solution chart, word wheel, cluster map, poetry grid, network tree, cause-and-effect map, SQ3R chart, T-chart, speech map, storyboard, story analysis chart, and more!

These brain-compatible activities are sure to engage and motivate every student's brain in your classroom! Watch your students change from passive to active learners as they process visual concepts into learning that is not only fun, but remembered for a lifetime.

Put It Into Practice

Lecture and repetitive worksheets have long been the traditional way of delivering knowledge and reinforcing learning. While some higher-achieving students may engage in this type of learning, educators now know that actively engaging students' brains is not a luxury, but a necessity if students are truly to acquire and retain content, not only for tests, but for life.

The 1990s were dubbed the Decade of the Brain, because millions of dollars were spent on brain research. Educators today should know more about how students learn than ever before. Learning style theories that call for student engagement have been proposed for decades, as evidenced by research such as Howard Gardner's theory of multiple intelligences (1983), Bernice McCarthy's 4MAT Model (1990), and VAKT (visual, auditory, kinesthetic, tactile) learning styles theories.

I have identified 20 strategies that, according to brain research and learning style theory, appear to correlate with the way the brain learns best. I have observed hundreds of teachers—regular education, special education, and gifted. Regardless of the classification or grade level of the students, exemplary teachers consistently use these 20 strategies to deliver memorable classroom instruction and help their students understand and retain vast amounts of content.

These 20 brain-based instructional strategies include the following:

1. Brainstorming and Discussion

2. Drawing and Artwork

3. Field Trips

4. Games

5. Graphic Organizers, Semantic Maps, and Word Webs

6. Humor

7. Manipulatives, Experiments, Labs, and Models

8. Metaphors, Analogies, and Similes

9. Mnemonic Devices

10. Movement

11. Music, Rhythm, Rhyme, and Rap

12. Project-based and Problem-based Instruction

13. Reciprocal Teaching and Cooperative Learning

14. Role Plays, Drama, Pantomimes, Charades

15. Storytelling

16. Technology

17. Visualization and Guided Imagery

18. Visuals

19. Work Study and Apprenticeships

20. Writing and Journals

This book features Strategy 5: Graphic Organizers, Semantic Maps, and Word Webs, and Strategy 18: Visuals. Both strategies integrate visual and verbal elements of learning. Picture thinking, visual thinking, and visual/spatial learning is the phenomenon of thinking through visual processing. Since 90% of the brain's sensory input comes from visual sources, it stands to reason that the most powerful influence on learners' behavior is concrete, visual images. (Jensen, 1994) Also, linking verbal and visual images increases students' ability to store and retrieve information. (Ogle, 2000)

Graphic organizers are visual representations of linear ideas that benefit both left and right hemispheres of the brain. They assist us in making sense of information, enable us to search for patterns, and provide an organized tool for making important conceptual connections. Graphic organizers, also known as word webs or semantic, mind, and concept maps, can be used to plan lessons or present information to students. Once familiar with the technique, students should be able to construct their own graphic organizers, reflecting their understanding of the concepts taught.

Because we live in a highly visual world, using visuals as a teaching strategy makes sense. Each day, students are overwhelmed with images from video games, computers, and television. Visual strategies capitalize specifically on the one modality that many students use consistently—the visual modality. Visuals include overheads, maps, graphs, charts, and other concrete objects that clarify learning. Since so much sensory input comes from visual sources, pictures, words, and artifacts around the classroom take on exaggerated importance in students' brains. Visuals such as these provide learning support and constant reinforcement.

These strategies help students make sense of learning by focusing on ways the brain learns best. Fully supported by the latest brain research, these strategies provide the tools you need to boost motivation, energy, and most important, the academic achievement of your students.

CHAPTER 1

Reading

Character Comparison: Venn Diagram

Skills Objectives

Use "compare and contrast" strategy for character analysis.
Use character traits to predict behavior.
Identify relevant details and key information.
Use language to connect and extend learning.

Materials

"The Intruder" reproducible

Character Comparison reproducible

A **Venn Diagram** is a graphic organizer that can help students compare and contrast almost anything, including characters in a story. Students can list character traits, evaluate character relationships, and recognize the literary element of character arc. Insights gathered by using a Venn diagram make characters easier to understand and visualize. This information can lead to a deeper understanding of literature in many ways. For example, once the diagram is complete, students should be able to predict behavior or identify the defining trait of each character. Recognizing how the author may have used character traits to develop the storyline or plot encourages students to be more involved readers.

1. Introduce the concept of "compare and contrast" by asking two volunteers to stand at the front of the class. Invite the rest of the class to compare and contrast the two students, for example: *Jenna has blue eyes, and Marco has brown eyes. Jenna and Marco are both 12 years old. Jenna likes reading fantasy books, and Marco likes mysteries. They both play soccer.*

2. Tell students that they are going to be using a Venn diagram to compare and contrast two characters in a story. Give students a copy of **"The Intruder"** and **Character Comparison reproducibles (pages 11–12)**. Read aloud the excerpt from "The Intruder." Tell students to pay close attention to the description of each character.

3. Initiate discussion by asking students to describe each character. Discuss traits that are physical as well as emotional. Ask questions such as: *Why do you think Alicia befriended*

Maya? Why doesn't Alicia like to be alone? Why would Alicia's parents leave them alone in the house?

4. Instruct students to use their Venn diagrams to closely examine each character's traits. Model for students on the board or an overhead by drawing a Venn diagram.

5. In the center of the Venn diagram (where the circles overlap), students will write traits that the characters share. For example: *They are girls; They go to Bryant Middle School; they live on the same street.* Write these traits in your diagram.

6. Students will write contrasting character traits in the outer circles. For example: *Alicia has long, dark hair; she makes friends easily; she's more timid. Maya has long, blonde hair; she doesn't make friends easily; she's bolder.* Write these traits in your diagram.

7. Then instruct students to work on their own to compare two characters from a book they're reading or have recently read. They can brainstorm ideas with a partner or work individually. Before they begin, make sure they understand how to record similar and contrasting ideas in the Venn diagram.

8. Once students complete their Venn diagrams, ask a couple of volunteers to share their work with the class. Point out which items in their diagrams are based on fact and which are based on opinion. Ask students to explain their thinking.

Extended Learning
- Ask students to continue the story in their own words. Have them describe what happens next.

- Ask students what character traits are most likely to change over time and which aren't. Have students explain their thinking.

- Have students choose one of their story characters and make a Venn diagram comparing themselves with the character.

- Have students draw a picture of each character. Encourage them to include details described in the story.

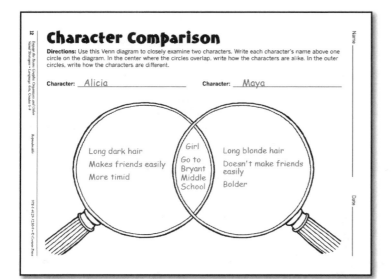

The Intruder

Alicia twisted Maya's long, blonde hair into a thick braid. The girls sat on the floor of Alicia's bedroom.

"Not like that," Maya complained. She studied the result in a mirror. "It's too loose. It looks stupid. See the hairs sticking out there."

Alicia smiled at the pouting girl. She was Maya's next-door neighbor and one of her only friends. Some of the other kids at Bryant Middle School did not seem to like Maya very much. "I'll use some clips. They'll look great."

Alicia pulled a sparkly clip from her own long, dark hair and started to redo the braid. Alicia's habit of looking for the best in people made her one of the most popular girls at school. She managed to get along with everyone, but Maya's moodiness was tricky. Tonight the alternative was staying home alone, which to Alicia was a fate worse than death. Both girls' parents would be at a parent-faculty meeting all evening.

Maya scowled. "It's no use. I just don't..."

Maya was interrupted by a loud, splintering sound from downstairs.

"What was that?" Alicia asked, alarmed. They both heard the crash of glass, like a window breaking. "Do you think it's your parents?" Her hands began to tremble.

Maya shook her head. "My parents would use a key." She stood up bravely. "I'm going downstairs to find out what's going on."

Alicia reached up and grabbed Maya's arm. "Please don't go downstairs; you don't know who's down there!" Both girls looked at each other, frozen with fear.

Character Comparison

Directions: Use this Venn diagram to closely examine two characters. Write each character's name above one circle on the diagram. In the center where the circles overlap, write how the characters are alike. In the outer circles, write how the characters are different.

Character:

Character:

Engage the Brain: Graphic Organizers and Other Visual Strategies • Language Arts, Grades 6–8   Reproducible   978-1-4129-5230-9 • © Corwin Press

A Way with Words: Word Map

Skills Objectives
Use context clues and prior knowledge to find word meaning.
Use dictionary skills.

Materials
A Way with Words reproducible

poem "Jabberwocky" by Lewis Caroll (optional)

To Kill a Mockingbird by Harper Lee (optional)

dictionaries

A well-developed vocabulary leads to better reading comprehension. A **Word Map** is a graphic organizer that helps students build their vocabulary. A word map can be used to list a main topic and related ideas, or words and their synonyms, antonyms, or definitions. In this activity, students build a collection of clues that help them retain learning and use vocabulary words in context. The word map works well as a pre-reading or postreading activity.

1. Read aloud the following passage from Lewis Caroll's "Jabberwocky":

   'Twas brillig, and the slithy toves
   Did gyre and gimble in the wabe;
   All mimsy were the borogoves,
   And the mome raths outgrabe.

   Beware the Jabberwock, my son!
   The jaws that bite, the claws that catch!
   Beware the Jubjub bird, and shun
   The frumious Bandersnatch!

2. Invite students to try to figure out what the nonsense words mean based on context clues (e.g., placement in the sentence, other recognizable words). Explain that challenging words may seem like nonsense words until students learn how to decipher them using context and other clues. A word map graphic organizer can help students decipher difficult words.

3. Give students a copy of the **A Way with Words reproducible (page 15)** and access to a dictionary.

4. Have students read a selection from a book or story of their choice, or use a book they are reading in class. For this activity, you may preselect a vocabulary list or ask students to generate a list as they read by jotting down words they don't know. The following sample word list is from *To Kill a Mockingbird* by Harper Lee: *assuage, apothecary, chattels, dictum, imprudent, piety, taciturn.*

5. Model how to use a word map on the board. Write a vocabulary word, such as *taciturn*, in the center book. Ask a volunteer

to guess what the word might mean from the context of the surrounding text, for example, *grumpy* or *lazy*. Write the answer in the book labeled *My Definition*.

6. Instruct students to look up the definition in the dictionary, for example: *Reserved or uncommunicative in speech, saying little.* Write it in the word map along with the part of speech, *adjective*. Compare the two definitions. Ask students: *Are the definitions alike? How does the definition help you understand the character?*

7. Encourage students to continue filling in the word map. Ask questions such as: *What words do you know that mean the same as **taciturn**? What words have the opposite meaning?* Invite a volunteer to think of an original sentence using the vocabulary word. For example: *Jake knew it would be difficult getting to know his taciturn neighbor.*

8. Once your word map is complete, direct students to choose a vocabulary word from their reading. Have them use that word to complete their word map.

Extended Learning

- Use the dictionary to find other forms of a word. For example, the adjective *taciturn* can be used as an adverb (*taciturnly*) or a noun (*taciturnity*). Prompt students to write an original sentence using each form of the word.

- Ask students if they know anyone who could be described as taciturn. Have students write or give oral examples of why this person fits this description.

- Use student word maps to generate a writing assignment. Encourage students to write a paragraph inspired by their word or its antonym.

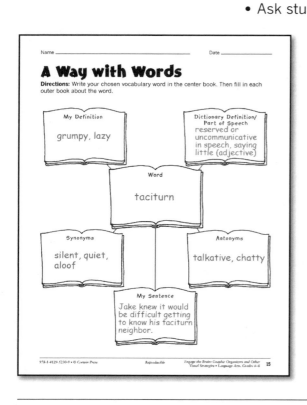

Name _____ Date _____

A Way with Words

Directions: Write your chosen vocabulary word in the center book. Then fill in each outer book about the word.

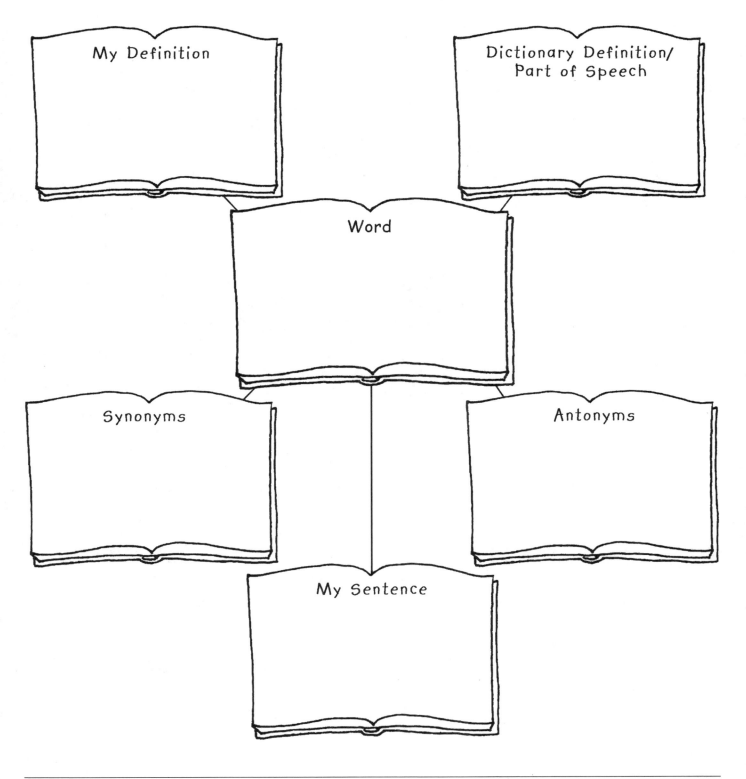

My Definition

Dictionary Definition/
Part of Speech

Word

Synonyms

Antonyms

My Sentence

A Place in Time: Timeline

Materials

A Place in Time reproducible

Anne Frank: The Diary of a Young Girl by Anne Frank (optional)

Skills Objectives

Identify relevant details and key information.
Visualize key moments in chronological order.
Draw conclusions based on prior knowledge.

A **Timeline** is a continuum that can be used in a variety of ways. For nonfiction, it is a straightforward means of allowing students to order events in chronological sequence. For fiction, it enables students to grasp relationships within a storyline, highlight important events in a character's life, or place a character in the proper historical context. Understanding the timeframe of a story helps the reader better understand character traits and behavior influenced by history, the passing of time, or cultural context.

1849: The California Gold Rush inspired the beginning of Westward Expansion. Sara knew her life would change forever.

1. Ask students what their lives would be like if they lived in the 1800s. For example: *Women could not vote; there were no televisions or computers; there were no airplanes or cars.* Then ask students how they have changed since kindergarten. *How have your interests changed? How have your bodies changed?* Guide students to see that time has a significant impact on a story.

2. Inform students that they will create a timeline based on a story but you will first be making a timeline together as a class. You may use a nonfiction or historical fiction book of your choice or this sample based on *Anne Frank: The Diary of a Young Girl.*

3. Give students a copy of the **A Place in Time reproducible (page 18)**, and then draw a similar timeline on the board. Explain that the first step in making a timeline is to determine the endpoints. Ask students: *Where should we start our timeline? Where should we end it?*

4. Begin the timeline with the birth of Anne Frank and end with the publication of her diary. Ask students to define the term *chronological order*. For example: *Putting events in order from the earliest to the most recent date*. Write each date on the timeline. Write the date above the line and the event below the line. Students can also use symbols or illustrations to show events.

5. Once students understand the concept of a timeline, they can make their own timelines based on a book or story they are reading. Explain that they may focus on a single chapter, a sequence of events from the story, or do a general timeline that covers the entire book.

6. Before students start independent work, check that they understand how to construct a timeline. Remind them to give the timeline an appropriate title, such as *Anne Frank: Birth to Publication.*

7. When students are finished with their timelines, invite volunteers to share how time affected or changed the characters or plot in their story.

8. Remind students that a timeline is a helpful tool for any subject matter. It is useful in social studies to track changes over time, such as the effects of the Industrial Revolution. It is also useful in science to show the progression of technology or certain inventions or discoveries.

Extended Learning

- Create a timeline of the historical period in which a story takes place. For example, for *Out of the Dust* by Karen Hesse, a student might do a timeline of the Dust Bowl period or the Great Depression.

- Have students create personal timelines of a period from their own lives.

- Discuss *setting* with students. Explain that the setting of a story includes more than just location. It also includes the time period and general environment. For example, a story might be set in Hawaii in 1872 during the rainy season. Discuss how setting might also be used to symbolize the emotional state of characters.

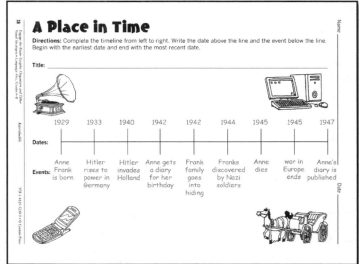

A Place in Time

Directions: Complete the timeline from left to right. Write the date above the line and the event below the line. Begin with the earliest date and end with the most recent date.

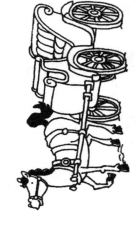

Title:

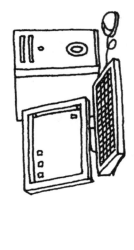

Dates:

Events:

Engage the Brain: Graphic Organizers and Other Visual Strategies • Language Arts, Grades 6–8   Reproducible   978-1-4129-5230-9 • © Corwin Press

Link by Link: Chain of Events Map

Skills Objectives

Identify main ideas.

Recognize cause-and-effect relationships.

Illustrate how text unfolds sequentially.

Materials

Link by Link reproducible

The Tell-Tale Heart by Edgar Allen Poe (optional)

overhead projector and transparency

A **Chain of Events Map** is an excellent post-reading tool that allows students to review information by showing it in steps or stages. It can help students describe a sequence of events or the actions of a character over a short or long period of time. This organizer guides students to visualize how one action or event leads to the next and, finally, to a logical outcome. A chain of events map also helps students organize their thoughts about what they are reading, distinguish the main ideas, and understand plot development.

1. Ask students what might happen if they didn't study for a test. They will say they probably wouldn't do very well. If they did not do well on the test, they might not pass the class. If they did not pass the class, they might not graduate. Explain that you have just described a chain of events. This chain shows how one event leads to the next.

2. Tell students they are going to describe the chain of events in a story. Give them a copy of the **Link by Link reproducible (page 21)**. Place a transparency of the reproducible on the overhead.

3. Select a short story or passage to model using the organizer, or use the short story *The Tell-Tale Heart* by Edgar Allen Poe. Begin by reading the story or poem aloud.

4. Ask students to determine which action or event sets off the chain of events. Explain that the answer should be as precise and active as possible. For *The Tell-Tale Heart*, ask students which of the following sentences describes the event that sets the story in motion: *The main character and the old man live in the same house*, or *the main character decides to kill the old man*. Lead students to see that the second sentence is more important to the plot of the story. Write it in the first link of the chain.

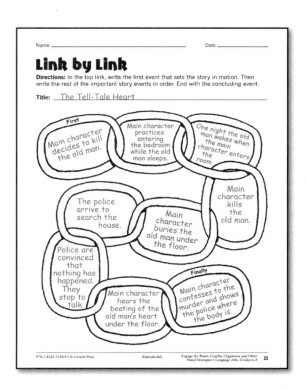

5. Encourage students to suggest other important events in the order they happened. List some of the events in the graphic organizer. Ask: *What events lead to the final outcome? What is the final outcome? How does one event lead to the next?* List several story events on the board, such as:

   1. *Main character decides to kill the old man.*
   2. *Main character practices entering the bedroom while the old man sleeps.*
   3. *One night the old man wakes when the main character enters the room.*
   4. *Main character kills the old man.*
   5. *Main character buries the old man under the floor.*
   6. *Police arrive to search the house.*
   7. *Main character hears the beating of a heart under the house.*
   8. *Main character confesses and shows the body to police.*

6. Point to the completed chain of events map. Ask students: *Are all of these events equally significant?* Explain that some events may not be as important to driving the plot as others. For example, events 1, 4, 6, and 8 are key events, while the others are supporting events.

7. Ask students if they understand how to fill in their graphic organizers. They should begin with the event that sets the story in motion and end with the concluding event. Instruct students to fill in their chain of events map based on a story or book they are currently reading. They can fill out the map for one chapter, one section, or the entire book.

8. When students are finished, ask volunteers to share how changing one event in their chain links might have created a different outcome to the story.

Extended Learning

- Have students work in small groups using their completed organizers. Tell groups to examine each student's organizer and decide on one event in the chain to change. Encourage them to discuss how that change may or may not influence the outcome and share their reasoning.

- Ask each student to write a different ending for their story and then work backward to make the events in the chain work logically with the new ending.

- Give students several old magazines. Direct them to create a visual chain of events using pictures from the magazines.

Link by Link

Directions: In the top link, write the first event that sets the story in motion. Then write the rest of the important story events in order. End with the concluding event.

Title: _____

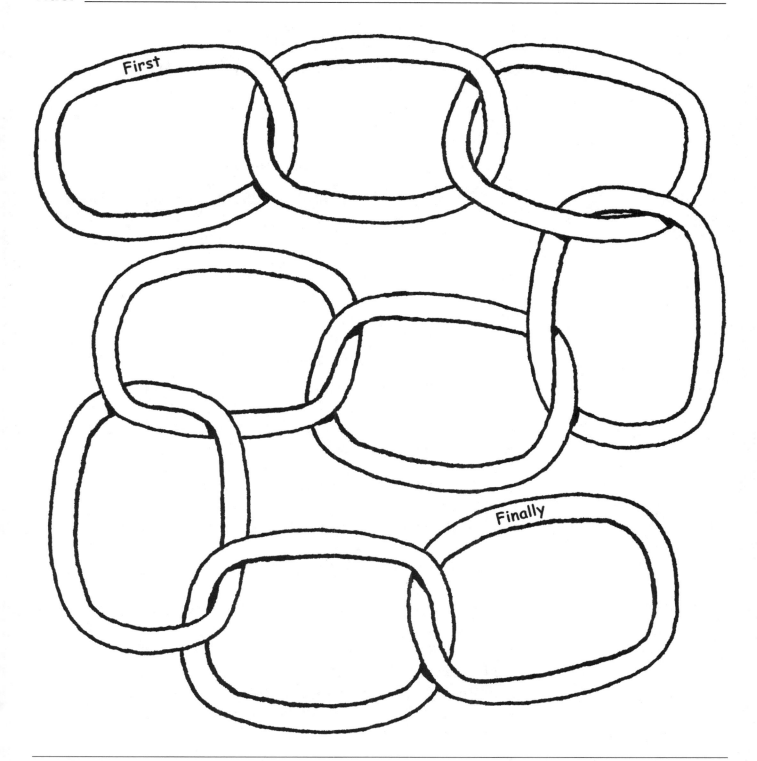

Down to the Bones: Fishbone Map

Materials

Down to the Bones
reproducible

Lord of the Flies
by William Golding
(optional)

Skills Objectives

Sort out relationships in complex ideas or events.

Recognize cause and effect.

Organize information in a hierarchy.

Students can use a **Fishbone Map** both during and after reading. This kind of graphic organizer allows them to structure ideas on a topic and make multifaceted information more manageable. It provides readers with a framework for recognizing the main idea and supporting details. This kind of map can be used to analyze a complex event, but it is flexible and can be adapted to suit the level of complexity of any text students are reading.

1. Give students a copy of the **Down to the Bones reproducible (page 24)**. Point out how the lines on the map are shaped like fish bones. Explain that this kind of graphic organizer can help them break down events in a story to find main ideas and supporting details.

2. Demonstrate how to fill out the map using the plot from a familiar book such as *Lord of the Flies* by William Golding. Discuss each character and what part he plays in the story. Invite students to share their ideas as well.

Sample Character List: *Lord of the Flies*

Ralph: Hunted by the boys; narrowly escapes being killed

Piggy: Smart but vulnerable; spectacles used to start fire; his death leaves Ralph alone

Sam and Eric: Twins loyal to Ralph; tribe captures them; won't tell where Ralph is hiding

Simon: Has insight and vision; understands that fear is unfounded; killed by the hunters

Jack: Ralph's rival and leader of the hunters; leads a revolt against Ralph; convinces his followers to destroy Ralph

Roger: Jack's cohort; cruel, sadistic boy; causes Piggy's death

Maurice: Easily led; supports Jack; helps steal Piggy's glasses

---

3. Explain that in the beginning of the book Ralph is the leader. At the end, he is running for his life from the tribe. At the "head" of the fish, write the main idea: *Ralph is hunted by the boys and narrowly escapes being killed.* Tell students you will be using the main characters to show how this plot change came about.

4. On the board, write the character names and key factors about each boy. Demonstrate how to complete the fishbone map so the most important characters and direct causes are closest to the head of the fish. Write the names of the characters on the diagonal lines.

5. Instruct students to consider each cause or influence for the change of plot and help you fill in two details about each one. Prompt them with *who, where, what, when* and *why* questions. Write character elements that led to the main event on the two horizontal "detail" lines associated with each name.

6. Discuss the finished organizer with students. Ask if they could add any details that would show how each character contributed to the plot of the story. Add more lines and details as needed.

7. Now invite students to use their fishbone map to organize main ideas and details, or story elements, about a book they are reading. Before they begin, make sure they understand that the main idea goes in the head of the fish and supporting details move from the front to the back in order of importance.

8. Display students' work on an ocean-themed bulletin board titled *A Sea of Ideas.* Encourage students to read classmates' fishbone maps to see how they organized ideas about their reading.

Extended Learning

- Invite students to consider how the end of the story might change if any elements changed. For example, in *Lord of the Flies*, what if several adults had also survived? What if the survivors were both girls and boys? All girls?

- Ask how the choices some characters make affect the other characters. Have student pairs perform a dialog to demonstrate this idea.

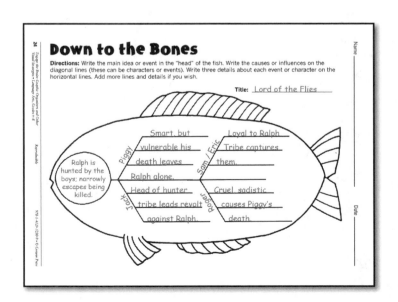

Down to the Bones

Directions: Write the main idea or event in the head of the fish. Write the causes or influences on the diagonal lines (these can be characters or events). Write three details about each event or character on the horizontal lines. Add more lines and details if you wish.

Title: _____

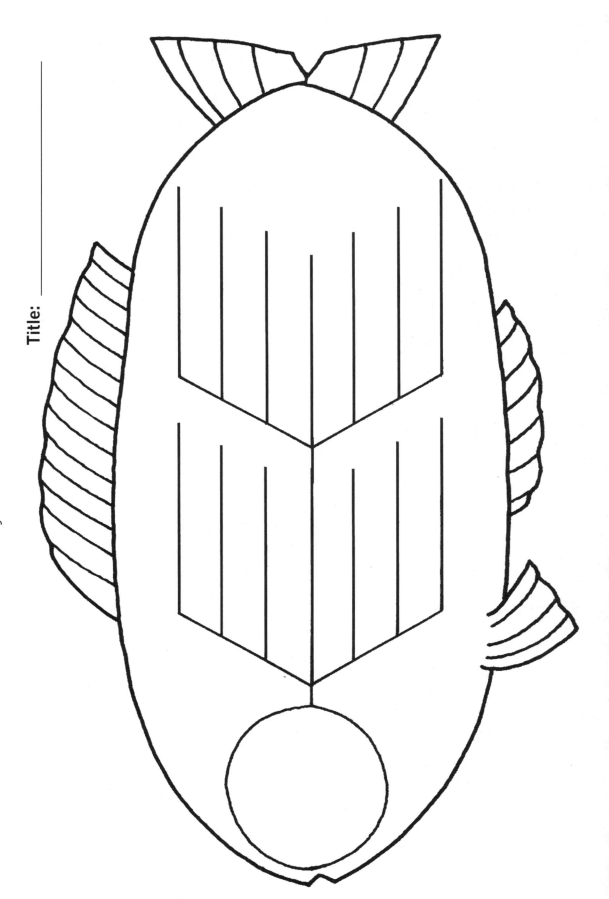

Rise and Fall: Story Analysis Chart

Skills Objectives
Understand plot structure.
Evaluate key points and conflict in a text.
Recognize theme.

Materials
Rise and Fall
reproducible

pictures of Egyptian
pyramids

overhead projector
and transparency
(optional)

A **Story Analysis Chart** is a postreading tool that helps students
identify the major elements of a story rather than focus on details. Using
this kind of organizer can increase overall comprehension by focusing
on the "big idea" or theme of the story. It is ideal for small group
discussions with peers.

1. Show students a picture of an Egyptian pyramid. Point out
   that pyramids were constructed by placing stones on top of
   one another. Each stone added to the balance of the structure.
   Tell students this is a good analogy for how stories are built.
   Each element is necessary to build a complete, balanced story:
   characters, setting, conflict, rising action, climax, falling action,
   and *resolution*.

2. Give students a copy of the **Rise and Fall reproducible (page 27)**.
   Introduce this organizer using a familiar story such as *Sleeping
   Beauty*. Retell the story or read a picture book version.

3. Model for students on the board, or place a transparency of the
   reproducible on the overhead. First, ask them to describe the
   setting of the story: *Where and when did the story take place?*
   Note anything unique about the setting, such as the season, time
   in history, or real or imaginary places.

4. Ask students to identify the protagonist and antagonist in the
   story. Explain that the antagonist is anyone or anything in conflict
   with the protagonist. It may be another person, an animal, nature,
   society, or fate. The conflict may also be internal. For this example,
   the protagonist would be *Sleeping Beauty (Briar Rose)* and the
   antagonist would be the *evil fairy*. Write these elements in
   your chart.

5. Explain that conflict is the main problem the protagonist must meet or solve. Complications that arise from this conflict are elements of rising action. Identify several examples, and discuss how each element adds to the story. In the *Conflict* section of the chart, write: *Evil fairy is not invited to the party. She curses the princess.* In the *Rising Action* section, write: *Good fairy softens the curse and hides the princess. Everyone in the kingdom falls asleep for 100 years.*

6. Point out how rising action moves up the pyramid to the peak, or climax, of the story and that the climax is rarely at the end of a story. It is the peak or turning point of the action. Encourage students to determine the turning point in *Sleeping Beauty*. In this case, it is the arrival of the prince and his fight to save Briar Rose.

7. Show students how to move down the other side of the pyramid to describe falling action and resolution. Help students understand falling action by asking: *What happens to the characters after the climax? Are there any explanations of the outcome? Does the author tie up any loose ends?* Write events that comprise falling action in the chart. Finally, write the resolution or ending: *The prince and Briar Rose live happily ever after.*

8. Explain that the theme is the main concept explored in the story. This element of the chart is most likely to promote a lively discussion.

9. Invite students to use their story analysis chart to analyze and list elements from a story they are currently reading. Before they begin, make sure they understand each element in the chart.

10. Invite students to share their charts in groups and focus on themes. Ask them to discuss whether they agree with the theme.

Extended Learning

- Have students write a short version of the story in a different setting. They can also try telling the story from the point of view of the antogonist.

- Discuss the different ways a story can end, such as closed, open, or with a cliffhanger. Ask students to keep a list of story endings for their own writing.

- Give students a supply of picture books and ask them to find the theme for each one.

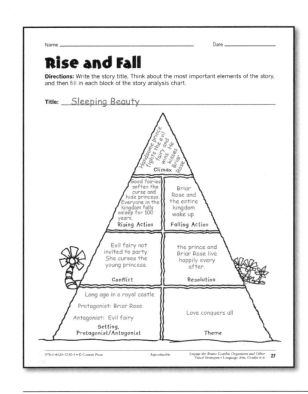

Name _____ Date _____

Rise and Fall

Directions: Write the story title. Think about the most important elements of the story, and then fill in each block of the story analysis chart.

Title: __Sleeping Beauty__

Handsome prince fights the evil fairy and kisses Briar Rose
Climax

Good fairies soften the curse and hide princess. Everyone in the kingdom falls asleep for 100 years. | Briar Rose and the entire kingdom wake up
Rising Action | Falling Action

Evil fairy not invited to party. She curses the young princess. | the prince and Briar Rose live happily every after.
Conflict | Resolution

Long ago in a royal castle
Protagonist: Briar Rose
Antagonist: Evil fairy
Setting, Protagonist/Antagonist | Love conquers all
Theme

978-1-4129-5230-9 • © Corwin Press   Reproducible   *Engage the Brain: Graphic Organizers and Other Visual Strategies • Language Arts, Grades 6–8*   27

Rise and Fall

Directions: Write the story title. Think about the most important elements of the story, and then fill in each block of the story analysis chart.

Title: _____

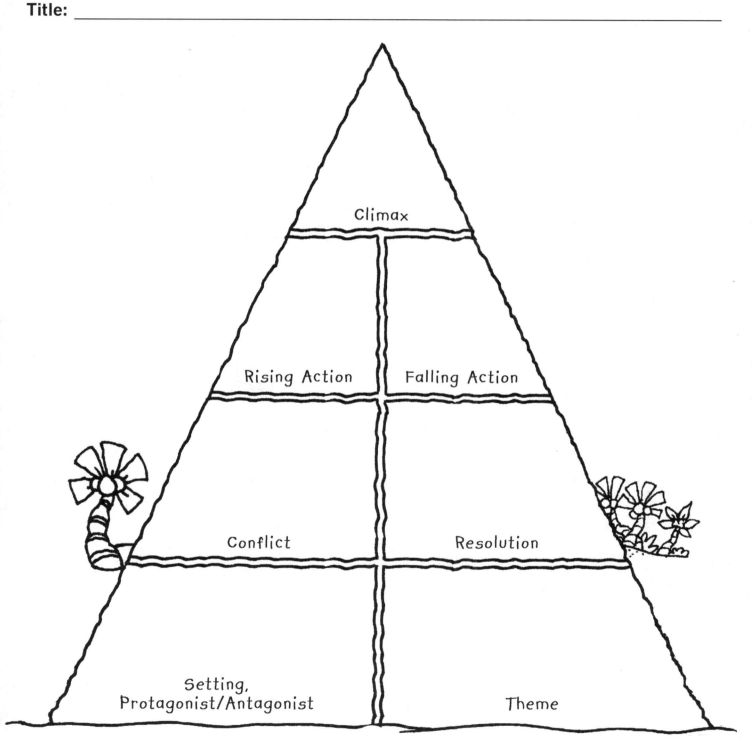

Climax

Rising Action   Falling Action

Conflict   Resolution

Setting,
Protagonist/Antagonist   Theme

Along Came a Spider: Spider Map

Materials

"All About Seals" reproducible

Along Came a Spider reproducible

nonfiction text passage

overhead projector and transparency

Skills Objectives

Read for a purpose.

Identify relevant details and key information.

Use reference materials to check for accuracy.

Access prior knowledge.

A **Spider Map** allows students to create a visual image of a central idea, process, or concept, and several subtopics associated with that idea. This map is helpful for reading nonfiction and organizing notes, and is a good choice if the information gathered does not fit into a hierarchy. It is equally useful as a study aid or organizational tool when preparing for a reading or writing assignment.

1. Read aloud a short passage from a nonfiction text. Tell students to take notes while you read. Ask students: *Are your notes easy to read? How can you organize your notes? What might make your notes easier to read?*

2. Give students a copy of the **"All About Seals"** and **Along Came a Spider reproducibles (pages 30–31)**. Place a transparency of the Along Came a Spider reproducible on the overhead.

3. Read aloud the article "All About Seals," or invite volunteers to read aloud each section. Then ask students to identify the big idea of the passage—seals. Write *seals* in the center circle of the spider map.

4. Then ask students to suggest subtopics to write on the diagonal lines extending from the center circle. Point out that four different seals are discussed in the article. These are the subtopics. Write

them on your map: *ringed seal, harbor seal, elephant seal,* and *leopard seal.*

5. As a class, choose and write two details for each subtopic. For example: *ringed seal—smallest true seal, lives farthest north; harbor seal—gathers in large groups, sometimes found in freshwater lakes; elephant seal—largest seal, lives in Antarctic; leopard seal—eats warm-blooded animals, females are larger than males.*

6. Make sure students understand how to fill out the spider map before assigning a passage for independent reading. Instruct students to read the passage first and then work with a partner to complete their spider map. Encourage them to add more subtopics and details to their map, if they wish.

7. When all the maps are complete, invite students to form small groups of two to three pairs. Direct them to discuss how each pair interpreted the reading.

Extended Learning

• Invite students to brainstorm what they already know about a nonfiction topic, such as volcanoes or skateboarding. Have them use different colored pens or pencils to help visually categorize information on the spider map. Explain that they should check each fact for accuracy. This encourages students to use prior knowledge and to investigate information.

• Have students write a short story or paragraph about their topic, incorporating what they have learned.

• Initiate a class discussion on ways the spider map could be used for fiction.

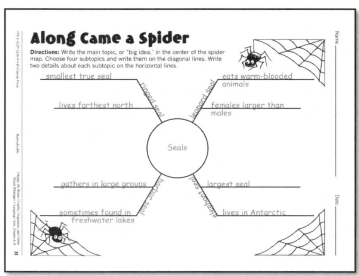

All About Seals

There are 18 species of seals in existence today. Seals, classified in a group called *pinnipeds*, can be found in all the world's oceans and a few freshwater lakes. Although all seals have some common characteristics, such as front and back flippers and a smooth torpedo shape, there are some big differences between various species.

At five feet long and 200 pounds, the ringed seal is the smallest true seal. It also lives the farthest north, foraging for fish and shellfish in the frigid Arctic waters. In winter, when bays and coastlines freeze over, the adult seal remains under sheets of ice. The ringed seal opens a hole large enough to haul itself out of the water for an occasional rest.

Harbor seals are the only true seals commonly found on both the Atlantic and Pacific coasts of North America. They are regular visitors to harbors and estuaries and may even travel upriver to freshwater lakes. In coastal waters, large groups of harbor seals bask in the sun on sandbars and rocky ledges. However, it is also common to sight a lone seal. This six-foot-long, 300-pound sea mammal is a strong, graceful swimmer; and for short distances, it can reach speeds of up to 18 miles per hour.

The southern elephant seal is the largest of all the pinnipeds. A male elephant seal grows up to 20 feet long and may weigh as much as four tons! The female rarely reaches half that size. The male also has a foot-long snout. When the huge male roars, he puffs up his snout and blasts forth an incredible call. The southern elephant seal lives in the Antarctic. When breeding time comes, the adult males gather on rocky island shores and coastal areas of Antarctica and the tip of South America. Each male stakes out a territory that he defends against other males. The females arrive soon after territories have been established.

The leopard seal is an excellent hunter. It prowls the cold waters of the Antarctic searching for food. This fierce seal is the only pinniped that regularly preys on warm-blooded animals such as penguins and other seals. Its powerful jaws are equipped with curved teeth to grasp its prey. The female is larger than the male. She may be 13 feet long and weighs about 840 pounds. The male is slightly smaller. Leopard seals are solitary animals. Males and females gather on certain Antarctic islands only during breeding season.

Along Came a Spider

Directions: Write the main topic, or "big idea," in the center of the spider map. Choose four subtopics and write them on the diagonal lines. Write two details about each subtopic on the horizontal lines.

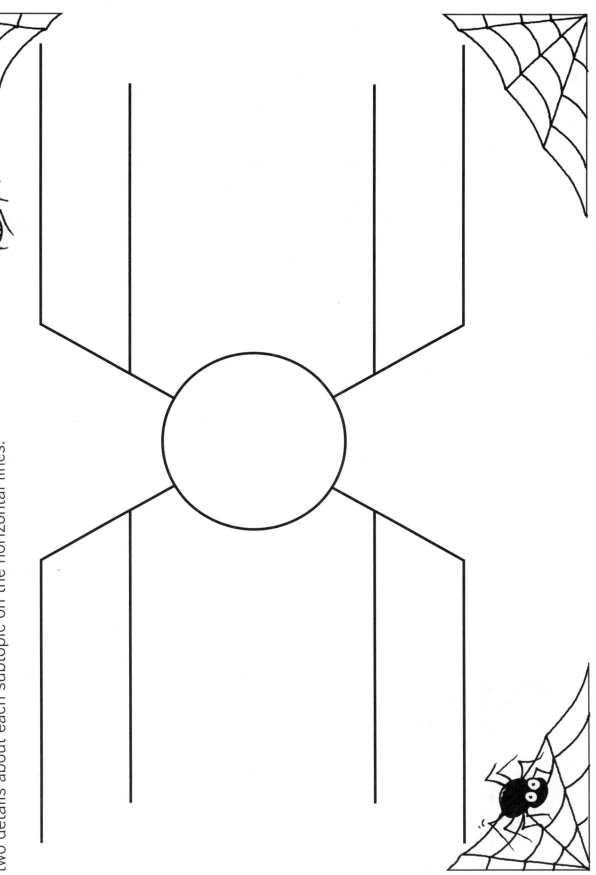

What's the Problem? Problem/Solution Chart

Materials

Problem/Solution Chart reproducible

short stories or fables

overhead projector and transparency

Skills Objectives

Identify main conflict.
Predict outcomes.
Recognize cause and effect.

The plot of a story usually centers on a problem or conflict between the protagonist and another character or element. Using a **Problem/Solution Chart** aids students in identifying the main conflict and examining how the protagonist succeeds or fails in dealing with a problem. This organizer is most effective when introduced while students are reading. This gives them the opportunity to identify the problem and brainstorm possible solutions to predict the outcome. This strategy encourages active rather than passive reading.

1. Discuss with students the framework of most of Aesop's fables, including "The Fox and the Grapes" and "The Lion and the Mouse." Usually, an animal character faces a conflict or challenge of some kind, and it learns a lesson. This lesson is called a *moral*. Read aloud the following fable:

   The Bat and the Weasels
   A Bat fell upon the ground and was caught by a Weasel. The Bat pleaded for the Weasel to spare his life. The Weasel refused, saying that he was by nature the enemy of all birds. The Bat assured him that he was not a bird, but a mouse. Thus, the Weasel set him free. Shortly afterward the Bat again fell to the ground and was caught by another Weasel. Again, the Bat begged the Weasel not to eat him. The Weasel said that he had a special hostility to mice. The Bat assured him that he was not a mouse, but a bat, and thus a second time he escaped.

2. Tell students they are going to analyze the problem and solution in a story. Give students a copy of the **Problem/Solution Chart reproducible (page 34)**. Make a transparency of the chart and place it on the overhead. Then model for students how to use the chart with the fable "The Bat and the Weasels."

3. Begin by writing the title and characters in the chart. Then read the fable aloud until you get to an obvious conflict. Ask students to determine the elements of the problem. Prompt them with questions such as: *What is the problem? Who is going to have to deal with it? Who or what is the cause of the problem? Why did it*

happen? For this fable, the answers might be: *The problem is that the Weasel wants to eat the Bat. The Bat will have to deal with it because he doesn't want to be eaten.*

4. Invite the class to suggest possible solutions and how they might be implemented. Discuss what the outcome might be for each. Have students predict the outcome of the fable. Then read on to see how the Bat attempted to save his life. Record the outcome on the chart.

5. Continue reading until you reach the Bat's next attempt to solve the problem. What does the Bat do this time? Write the final outcome on the chart. Compare students' predictions and discuss why the protagonist chose the solution that led to that outcome. Ask students: *Was it in fact the best possible answer?*

6. Have students read a short story to the point at which a conflict arises and then fill in the first few sections of the problem/solution chart. Tell them to continue to read and fill in the chart, recording attempts to solve the problem and their outcomes. Finally, have them complete the story and record the solution. Make sure students understand that this chart should be completed during reading, not after, so they can record the events and predict the outcome.

7. When students' charts are complete, ask how many students predicted the correct solution. Ask if their own solution might have solved the problem just as well. Invite students to share their thoughts.

Extended Learning

- Have students choose an alternative solution to the problem in their story. Ask them to use it to rewrite the story's ending.

- Encourage the class to think about what happened to the protagonist at the end of the story. Ask: *How has he or she changed?* Have students reflect about the character in their journals.

- Have students plan a story starting with the end result and working backward. Provide a prompt such as: *What if you saw someone throwing a computer over a cliff? What sort of problem do you think may have led to such a drastic solution? What type of character would take such an action?*

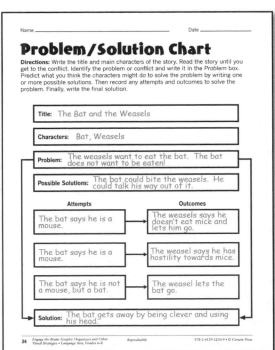

Problem/Solution Chart

Directions: Write the title and main characters of the story. Read the story until you get to the conflict. Identify the problem or conflict and write it in the *Problem* box. Predict what you think the characters might do to solve the problem by writing one or more possible solutions. Then record any attempts and outcomes to solve the problem. Finally, write the final solution.

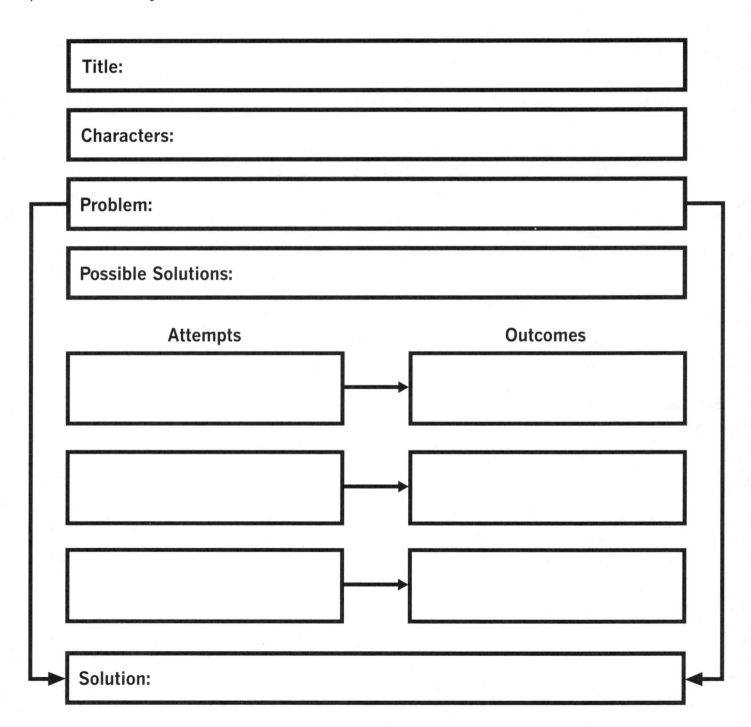

Title:

Characters:

Problem:

Possible Solutions:

Attempts   Outcomes

Solution:

CHAPTER 2

Writing

Quite a Character! Character Pyramid

Skills Objectives
Use character traits to predict behavior.
Identify relevant details and key information.
Use precise adjectives.

Materials
Character Pyramid reproducible

Strong characters are one of the most important elements of a well-written story. Student writers can better understand the main character's goals and motivations by completing a **Character Pyramid** for their protagonist. A character pyramid helps to clarify point of view and creates a template for students to revisit as the story develops. This organizer also allows student writers to develop story characters that are well-rounded and dynamic rather than flat and static.

1. Ask students what traits create a good main character, or protagonist, in a book. Students might respond with traits such as: *courageous, intelligent, funny, charming*, and so on. Challenge students to think of negative, quirky, and unusual traits, as well. List responses on the board.

   Possible Character Traits
   bold, brave, bully, creative, shy, friendly, studious, courageous, antagonistic, lazy, attractive, selfish, cheerful, humble, independent, pushy, short, sensible, curious, inventive, poor, energetic, funny, respectful, considerate, calm, messy, wealthy, tall, athletic, sneaky, generous, naughty, dynamic, heroic, nasty, careless, clever, bossy, loving, protective, honest, successful, cruel, intelligent, beautiful, lucky, neat, reliable, dangerous, repulsive, anxious, gloomy, jolly, troubled, reckless, agreeable, confused, stubborn, foolish

2. Inform students that they will be writing a short story based on a main character. The first element they will work on is character development. Suggest some of the traits listed on the board. Give students a copy of the **Character Pyramid reproducible (page 37)**. Then draw a simple pyramid on the board, using the reproducible as a guide.

3. As a class, come up with a physical description of a sample character. Point out that rich, specific details can make a character more vivid and alive to the reader. Ask students: *Is there something unusual about this character's appearance? What makes this character stand out?* Offer suggestions such as *very tall, fiery red hair,* or *an interesting scar.* Write ideas in your chart.

4. Next, build a personality for the character. Remind students that nobody's perfect, so the character should display both positive and negative traits. Suggest that someone who is kind and generous might also be a little lazy, or the grumpy man next door may be very kind to animals. Write several ideas in your chart.

5. Then ask students to suggest a talent or talents that the character might have. Perhaps she can blow a perfect bubble with bubblegum, or he can sing beautifully.

6. Next, invite students to make suggestions about the character's goals, which will drive the story. Ask: *What does this character want more than anything else in the world? What must he or she do to achieve these goals? What is one thing the character has already accomplished? What is one thing the character regrets?*

7. Complete the pyramid by having students decide on a name for the character. Mention that a name can create an image, such as a weightlifter named Petunia or a tiny dog named Apollo. These names imply certain traits about the character.

8. Have students work with partners to develop their own character pyramid. Remind them to fill in each section with both positive and negative traits to create multi-faceted, interesting characters.

9. Invite students to individually write a short story about the character. When they are finished, have pairs meet again to compare and contrast their stories.

Extended Learning

- Use a character pyramid to profile an antagonist. After the protagonist and antagonist have both been profiled, ask students to write a dialogue between the two characters.

- Instruct students to write a one-paragraph scene about their protagonist in a variety of circumstances, such as being trapped in a haunted house, finding a secret passageway, or training for a competitive race.

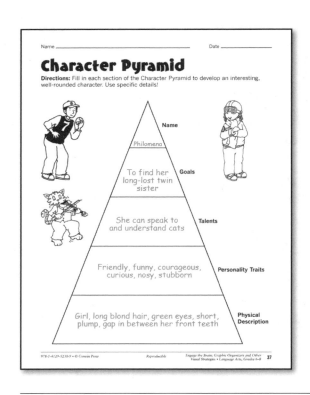

Name _____   Date _____

Character Pyramid

Directions: Fill in each section of the Character Pyramid to develop an interesting, well-rounded character. Use specific details!

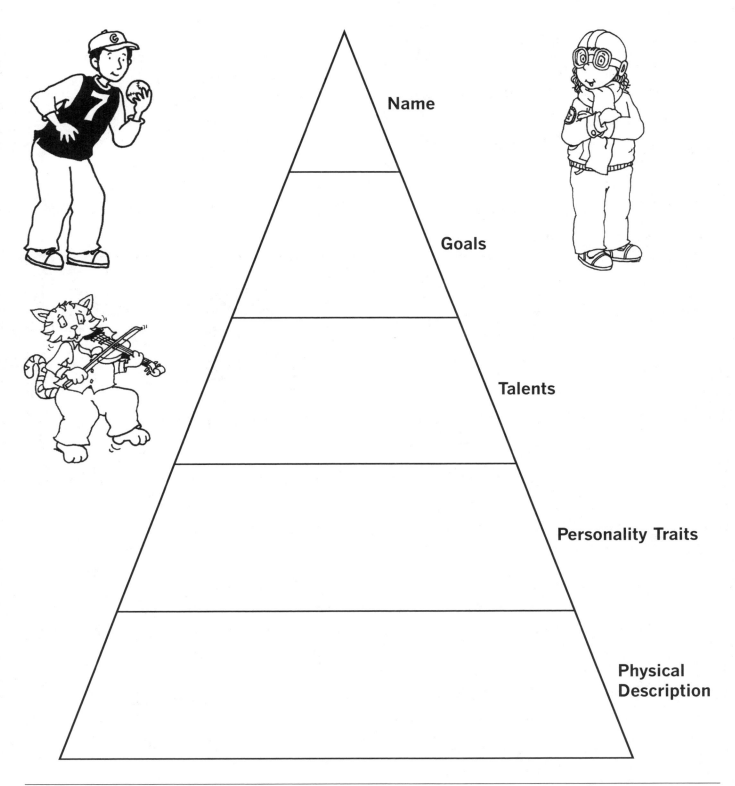

Name

Goals

Talents

Personality Traits

Physical Description

Picture This! Storyboard

Materials

Picture This! Storyboard reproducible

graphic book or comic book

old magazines

scissors

glue

crayons, markers, colored pencils

Skills Objectives

Understand the sequential process.

Visualize a story in chronological order.

Summarize a story.

Illustrate a story concept.

A **Storyboard** is a visual outline of a narrative. As a prewriting activity, it is useful for organizing ideas and sequencing action. It enables the writer to summarize a plot in the visual equivalent of sound bites. By illustrating the important events in a story, students can see what works and what doesn't before committing ideas to paper.

1. Show students a graphic novel or comic book. Point out that the the depiction of each scene in each box, or cell, is similar to a storyboard. Explain that a storyboard shows snapshots of all the events in a storyline.

2. Prepare students for drawing their own storyboard with a cut-and-paste activity using old magazines. Propose a simple story such as *A Family Trip*. Have students look through the magazines and cut out four pictures that show their interpretation of that story. For example: a family in a car, a photo of a beach, kids playing in the surf, a child sleeping in bed. Instruct them to paste or tape the pictures in two rows of two each and to number the pictures in story order. Display a couple of students' magazine stories and discuss them as a class.

3. Give students a copy of the six-cell **Picture This! Storyboard reproducible (page 40)**. Encourage students to brainstorm a simple story idea and think of the six major events that take place. The

first pair should relate to the opening and rising action. The second pair should relate to the climax, and the last pair should relate to the falling action and resolution. Point out that details are less important than the main events of the storyline.

4. Have students draw each main event of their story in the storyboard. Some students will feel more comfortable drawing than others. Assure them that the exercise is about plot development rather than artistic skill.

5. Once storyboards are complete, encourage students to write details about the story on another sheet of paper.

6. To close the activity, divide the class into groups so they can share their storyboards. Spend some time with each group to model how to give constructive, positive comments. Once the critique process is complete, give each student time to write a first draft of a story based on his or her storyboard.

Extended Learning

• Tell students that a comic strip is much like a storyboard. Invite them to bring in examples of comic strips or draw their own.

• Have students read a short story and then draw a storyboard for it.

• After lunch, invite students to draw a storyboard about something that happened during the break.

Name _____   Date _____

Picture This! Storyboard

Directions: Think of a story you would like to tell. Draw the six most important scenes in the storyboard. Number each cell of your storyboard in order. Include scenes for the opening, rising action, climax, falling action, and resolution of the story.

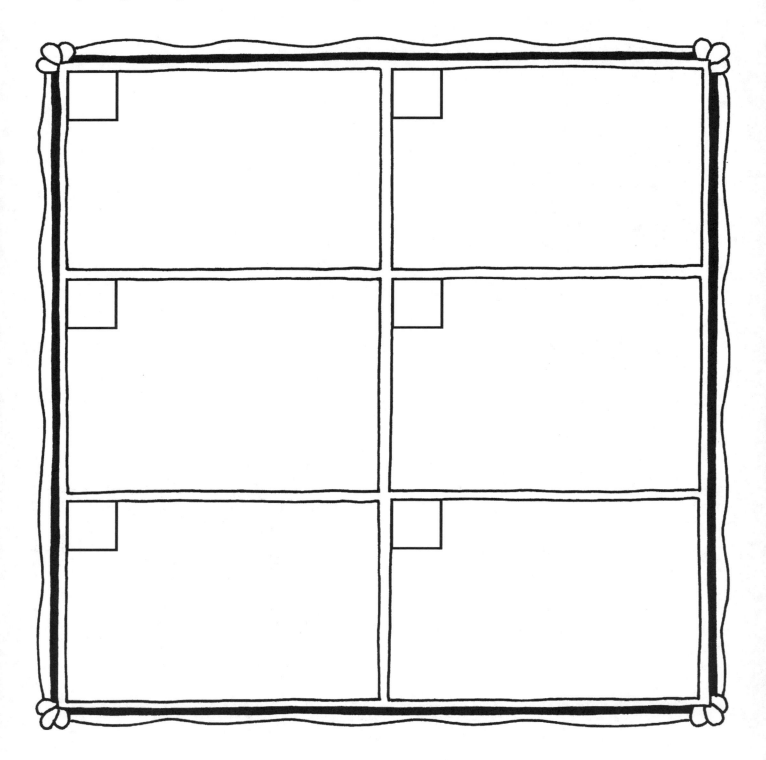

Engage the Brain: Graphic Organizers and Other   Reproducible   978-1-4129-5230-9 • © Corwin Press
Visual Strategies • Language Arts, Grades 6–8

From Here to There: Nonfiction Flowchart

Skills Objectives
Understand the purpose of nonfiction.

Identify key facts.

Sequence and summarize events in an article.

Materials

From Here to There reproducible

examples of "how-to" writing (recipes, instructions)

overhead projector and transparency (optional)

Whether students are writing fiction or nonfiction, structure is a key element. A **Nonfiction Flowchart** allows a writer to visualize the basic rhythm of nonfiction. It helps students to organize observations and opinions, recognize key points, and avoid straying from the central focus. By following a simple nonfiction flowchart, a writer can create a clear, easy-to-follow sequence in an article or other passage. This chart is particularly useful for writing instructions.

1. Begin by reading aloud several examples of "how-to" writing to students, such as recipes or instructions for how to fix a bike or play a game. Encourage students to take notes while you read to identify key information. After reading, ask: *What do you remember most about the piece? Why did it get your attention? Do you think you could complete the task described? Why or why not?*

2. Give students a copy of the **From Here to There reproducible (page 43)**. Then brainstorm a simple how-to topic as a class. The topic can be comical, such as *how to recognize an alien*, or basic, such as *how to ride a bicycle*. Point out that how-to articles use a modified problem–solution structure.

3. Draw a flowchart on the board, or place a transparency of the From Here to There reproducible on the overhead. Identify the goal of your class how-to, and use that goal to title the chart. For example: *How to Grow Tomatoes*.

4. Point out that each box in the flowchart is on a road, the road that leads from the beginning to the end of the article. On the road next to each square, students can suggest examples, special tips, or opinions that support or clarify the main points or steps. Such elements will add interest and make the finished work more appealing. However, it's very important that these tips not distract or wander from the main points.

5. Ask students to help you come up with six important steps in the process, and write one in each box—*First, Next, Then, After that, And then*, and *Finally*. For example: *First, buy tomato seeds. Next, prepare the soil with fertilizer. Then, plant the seeds. After that,*

water the seeds regularly. (In the road next to the *And then* box, write: *Make sure not to overwater!*) *And then, tie the small plant to a stake to keep it upright. Finally, harvest your tomatoes.*

6. When you are finished demonstrating how to use the flowchart, initiate a class discussion to give students ideas for their own how-to articles. Encourage students to consider not only practical, straightforward how-to's, but also humorous ones. Ask questions such as: *Do you play a sport? How might you explain to someone how to play this sport? Do you have a pet? How do you train a dog to speak? How do you throw a birthday party for a cat?* Suggest creative, adventurous ideas as well, such as how to find a hidden treasure or how to travel back in time to the Middle Ages.

7. Finally, have students write a how-to article, beginning with their flowchart. Make sure students understand how to complete the flowchart, and assist as needed. After they complete the flowchart, they can move on to writing each step as its own paragraph to create an article.

8. When students are finished with their articles, invite them to peer-edit with partners. Have partners read and critique each other's work. They can look for simple things such as punctuation and grammar, as well as content-related things such as clarity of the steps, relevance of the details, and overall comprehensibility of the instructions

Extended Learning

- Suggest that illustrations can enhance the flow of nonfiction text. Ask students to create an illustration showing each step.

- Have students use the flowchart for a biography of someone they know or an autobiography of their own lives.

- Invite small groups to choose one of their how-to articles to act out or demonstrate for the class.

Name _____   Date _____

From Here to There

Directions: Write the title of your "how-to" article. Think about how you will explain the process, step by step. Fill in the flowchart, starting with the first step. Use space in the road to fill in any important details, tips, or further explanation.

Title: How to Grow Tomatoes

First Buy tomato seeds.

Next Prepare the soil with fertilizer.

Then Plant the seeds.

After that Water the seeds regularly. Make sure not to overwater!

And then Tie the small plant to keep it upright.

Finally Harvest your tomatoes.

978-1-4129-5230-9 • © Corwin Press   Reproducible   *Engage the Brain: Graphic Organizers and Other Visual Strategies • Language Arts, Grades 6–8*   **43**

From Here to There

Directions: Write the title of your how-to article. Think about how you will explain the process step by step. Fill in the flowchart, starting with the first step. Use space in the road to fill in any important details, tips, or further explanation.

Title: _____

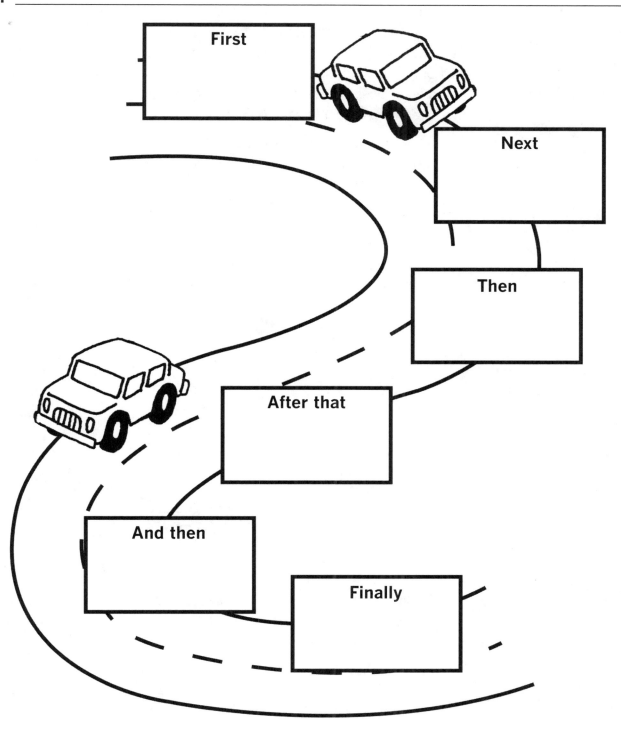

First

Next

Then

After that

And then

Finally

Brainstorming: Cluster Map

Materials

Brainstorming Cluster Map reproducible

old necklace (or other object of interest)

overhead projector and transparency (optional)

Skills Objectives

Use figurative language.

Integrate various concepts.

Incorporate imagery into text.

When a writer is searching for inspiration, a **Cluster Map** can really get the creative juices flowing! Clustering is a nonlinear process and naturally encourages lateral thinking. It can stimulate words and images around a key word or topic without interfering with the stream of ideas. Through word and idea associations, students get a visual map of the creative process that leads to imaginative plot development. This simple tool can help students see connections that might otherwise be missed.

1. Hold up an object for the class, such as a necklace. Tell students you found the necklace by a bench in the park. Since there was no lost and found, you took the necklace home. Ask students: *To whom do you think the necklace belongs? How did he or she lose the necklace? Who bought the necklace, and why? Was it a family heirloom that belonged to a great-great grandmother, or was it a birthday gift?* Encourage students to keep thinking about where the necklace came from until they begin building a story around it.

2. Give students a copy of the **Brainstorming Cluster Map reproducible (page 46)**. Explain that this kind of graphic organizer can be used to record and organize a free flow of ideas.

3. Model how to use the map by thinking up a mystery story focused around the necklace. Draw a cluster map on the board, or place a transparency of the reproducible on the overhead.

4. Begin with a single word, such as *necklace*. Write it in the center oval of the map. (You could also write a person, phrase, or action.) Remind students that you are planning to write a mystery story. Guide them by asking: *What happened to the necklace?* Ask them to think of as many spontaneous, single-word responses as they can. In the ovals around the key word, write four responses. If a student suggests the necklace was eaten, add it to the list!

5. Guide students by saying: *Now, let's think about who is responsible for the missing necklace. If it was eaten, who or what ate it?* Write responses for *eaten* in the three connecting ovals. For example: *dog, wood chipper, garbage disposal*.

6. Once the map is completed, allow students time to study the map. Then start looking for connections. Draw lines between ideas that work together. Ask questions such as: *How did the necklace end up in the wood chipper?* Give students about 15 minutes to write a simple outline for a mystery story based on the ideas in your cluster map. Invite volunteers to share their outlines.

7. Remind students how to record and connect ideas in the map. Make sure students understand how to use the map to build a story. Then instruct them to work with a partner to think of an original story concept by filling in their own cluster map. Have them use colored pencils or markers to circle ideas that work together.

Extended Learning

- Give students another copy of the Brainstorming Cluster Map reproducible, and then play some music. Invite students to freely associate words or feelings with the music and record their ideas in the map.

- Have students use a cluster map to brainstorm ideas about a character's likes, dislikes, talents, goals, quirks, and dreams.

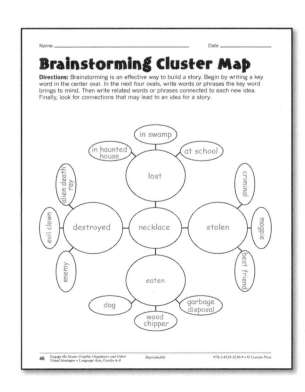

Brainstorming Cluster Map

Directions: Brainstorming is an effective way to build a story. Begin by writing a key word in the center oval. In the next four ovals, write words or phrases the key word brings to mind. Then write related words or phrases connected to each new idea. Finally, look for connections that may lead to an idea for a story.

翻印。時候貼起来!

Pulling It All Together: Literature Cycle

Skills Objectives
Demonstrate knowledge of story elements.
Understand the circular structure of a story, and how one event leads to the next.
Identify relevant details and key information.

Materials
Literature Cycle reproducible

overhead projector and transparency

Similar to the story analysis chart, a **Literature Cycle** gives young writers a visual overview of their entire story. It requires students to consider the literary elements of characters, setting, and theme as a whole, as well as the cycle of events. It is helpful for students to use the literature cycle in tandem with a cluster map so they can generate a flow of ideas if they are uncertain about any element of the story.

1. Ask a volunteer to tell you the plot of a popular movie. Ask students: *What was the problem or conflict? How did the characters solve the problem? How did one event lead to the next?* After students describe the plot, explain that movies have all the same elements of a story.

2. Inform students that they will be writing an original story. Give them a copy of the **Literature Cycle reproducible (page 49)**, and place a transparency of the reproducible on the overhead. Take time to review the graphic organizer. Point out that the cycle of events flows in a circular pattern. Often a story will move from one event to the next, and then end up back where it started.

3. For the purpose of discussion begin with characters. Ask students: *Who is your main character? Who or what is your antagonist? What other characters might appear in your story?* Invite students to offer suggestions, such as *the funny cat lady down the street, the class bully, the courageous firefighter, my sneaky little brother,* or *the computer genius.* Invite students to write their favorite ideas in their literature cycle.

4. Then move on to setting. Encourage students to think about three elements: time, place, and environment. For example: *It's the turn of the century in a small English town.* Invite students to offer creative ideas while you jot them on the transparency.

5. When you address theme, ask students: *What is the underlying message or big idea of the story?* Examples might include: *Love conquers all; enjoy life while you can;* or *true friendship is invaluable.* Theme is often the most difficult element for young

writers to identify. However, if you begin with a theme or provide several choices, students enjoy building a story around it!

6. Then direct students' attention to the beginning of the cycle—*Opening Line*. Explain that the opening line of a story is meant to draw the reader in and make them want to continue reading. Read aloud samples of excellent opening lines from various books. For example:

   • *Where's Poppa going with that axe?* from *Charlotte's Web* by E. B. White
   • *There is no lake at Camp Green Lake* from *Holes* by Louis Sachar
   • *It was a bright cold day in April, and the clocks were striking thirteen* from *1984* by George Orwell
   • *Not every thirteen-year-old girl is accused of murder, brought to trial, and found guilty. But I was just such a girl, and my story is worth relating even if it did happen years ago* from *The True Confessions of Charlotte Doyle* by Avi

   Discuss with the class why these opening lines are appealing and interesting and draw you into the story.

7. After students think of characters, a setting, and a theme, they can work on the cycle of events. Explain that each event should lead logically to the next. When students are done listing events, they can title their story. A good title should give an idea of what the story is about.

8. Give students some time to think about their story ideas. Allow them to go back and make revisions as needed. Walk around the class and prompt students with leading questions if they seem stuck.

9. Once students' literature cycles are complete, instruct students to write an original story based on their ideas. Allow them to illustrate their stories and compile them in a class book.

Extended Learning

• Provide picture books or short stories, and have students use them to complete a literature cycle.

• Ask students to consider what elements they might add to the literature cycle if they were writing a fantasy, mystery, fairy tale, tall tale, fable, or ghost story.

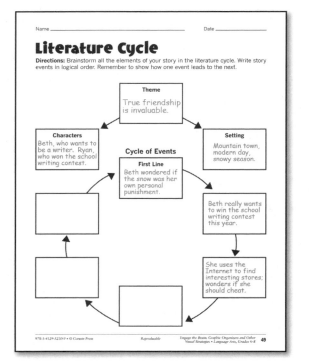

Literature Cycle

Directions: Brainstorm all the elements of your story in the literature cycle. Write story events in logical order. Remember to show how one event leads to the next.

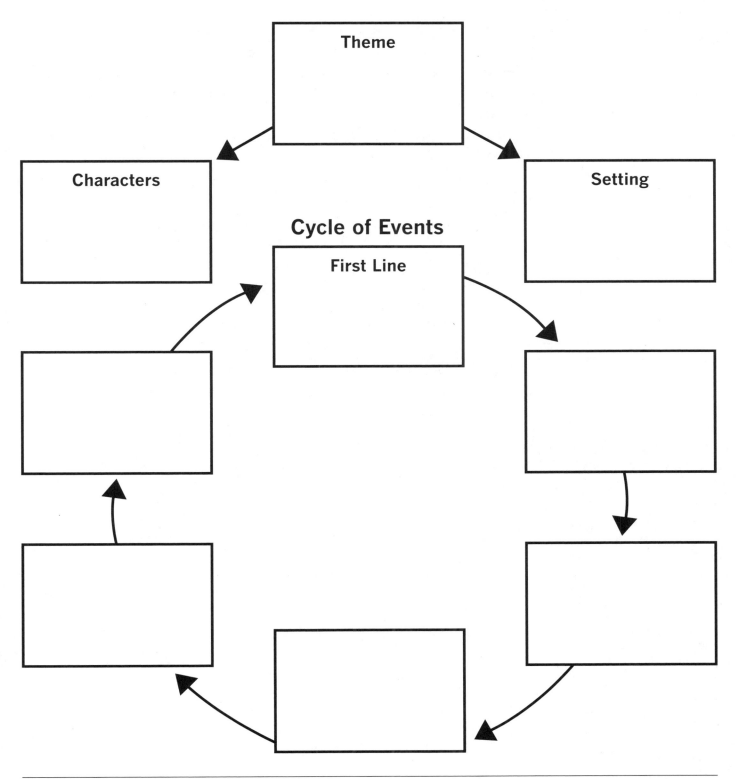

Theme

Characters

Setting

Cycle of Events

First Line

So That's Why It Happened!
Cause-and-Effect Map

Materials

"Transcontinental" reproducible

So That's Why It Happened! reproducible

Skills Objectives

Think and write in a logical sequence.
Predict a result.

Following cause-and-effect relationships encourages young writers to think critically and recognize plausible conclusions. **Cause-and-Effect Maps** graphically illustrate how story elements are linked. They allow students to explore the way a character's actions affect other characters or events around them. This graphic organizer can highlight incorrect or nonsensical connections and give the writer a clear picture of weaknesses in story structure.

1. Begin the lesson by demonstrating the concept of cause and effect. It can be as simple as flipping the light switch so the classroom dims. Ask students to look outside. Ask: *Are there clouds in the sky? Is it rainy or sunny?* Explain that weather is the result of causes that are fairly well understood. When gray clouds gather (*cause*), rain is usually the result (*effect*). Ask students: *How can you apply cause and effect to your writing? For example, what do you think would happen if one character spread a rumor about another? What might be the effect?*

2. Give students a copy of the **"Transcontinental"** and **So That's Why It Happened! reproducibles (pages 52–53)**. Peak students' interest by asking: *How could a girl's sneeze in Los Angeles cause a total stranger in New York to cry?*

3. Read aloud the story "Transcontinental" while students follow along at their desks, or invite volunteers to read it aloud.

4. Tell students you will work as a group to fill out a cause-and-effect map on the board. Draw a simple map based on the reproducible. Begin by asking: *What started the series of events in the story? Was it Charla's birthday party?* Go through the story step by step, pointing out causes and effects, until students can make the connections between a sneeze in Los Angeles and tears in New York. Fill in the chart as you go along.

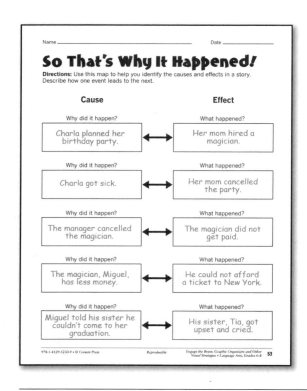

5. Tell students they will write their own cause-and-effect story using their cause-and-effect map. This map will help them outline the events that lead up to the final conclusion and make logical connections along the way.

6. Before students get started, make sure they understand that each cause must have an effect and vice versa. Whey they're finished, invite volunteers to read their maps aloud to the class but stop just before the last effect. Allow the class to guess the final result.

Extended Learning

• Ask students to examine their completed cause-and-effect maps. Ask them how the outcome would have changed if one of the causes had changed. Invite them to fill out a new map based on this change.

• Have students bring in newspaper articles that illustrate cause and effect. As a class, identify each cause and effect in the articles. Then bind the articles into a book for future reference. Students can refer to this book to get story ideas!

• Make a list of effects and ask students to imagine what might be the cause in each case. For example: *The boy dropped his ice-cream cone because...; The island cruise was a disaster because...; The dog started growling because...; The baby was crying because...*

Transcontinental

Charla couldn't wait for Saturday to arrive! It was her birthday, and she would be celebrating at Swirling Seas with ten of her friends. It was the biggest water park in Los Angeles. Her mom had even planned to hire a magician to do tricks at the party.

"Is something wrong?" her friend Min asked on Friday morning. "You look pale."

"I'm feeling kind of queasy," Charla admitted. "I've been so busy planning for the party; I'm probably just not getting enough sleep." By midmorning Charla felt hot and her throat was sore. Mr. Brooks sent her to the school nurse.

"I'll be okay," she moaned when her mother picked her up from school. Charla sneezed and wiped her reddening nose with a tissue.

"I'm sorry," her mom soothed. "I think you are too sick to spend the day at the water park. We will have to cancel the party. Don't worry. We'll plan something else when you're feeling better."

After tucking Charla in bed at home, her mom called the water park to cancel the party. Then she called the magician to cancel as well.

Miguel Hernandez was a college student. He made extra money as a magician performing at parties and other special events. Miguel was sorry to hear that Charla was sick. He was also sorry he wouldn't be performing at the party, because that meant he wouldn't be able to afford the airfare to New York next weekend. It was his sister Tia's graduation. Sadly, he dialed Tia's number on his cell phone.

"Miguel?" Tia answered happily. "Do you have your schedule yet? When are you getting here?"

"Tia," Miguel said slowly, picturing her wide grin. "I'm sorry, but I won't be able to make it." He could sense her smile fading as he spoke. "My plans fell through. I guess we'll have to wait for winter break."

"Okay," Tia said softly. "I understand. I'm just sorry I won't see you." They talked for a few minutes then said good-bye. Tia hung up the phone and wiped away her tears.

So That's Why It Happened!

Directions: Use this map to help you identify the causes and effects in a story. Describe how one event leads to the next.

Cause		Effect
Why did it happen?		What happened?
	⟷	
Why did it happen?		What happened?
	⟷	
Why did it happen?		What happened?
	⟷	
Why did it happen?		What happened?
	⟷	
Why did it happen?		What happened?
	⟷	

Build It! Paragraph Chart

Materials

"A Space Pioneer" reproducible

Built It! reproducible

sandwich ingredients such as bread, lettuce, meat, cheese, tomato (optional)

overhead projector and transparency

Skills Objectives

Recognize the main idea.

Identify relevant details and key information.

Understand paragraph structure.

A well-written essay presents a clear picture of the writer's vision. The paragraph is the basic unit of the essay, so paragraph structure is particularly important. The sandwich-style **Paragraph Chart** provides students with a fun and interesting way to remember the main elements of a paragraph. It can also help reinforce the organizational patterns required to write a competent five-paragraph essay, a standard measure of writing proficiency.

1. Draw a picture of a sandwich on the board, or use the elements of a real sandwich. Ask students to identify each part of the sandwich: *bread*, *meat*, *cheese*, *lettuce*, *tomato*, and so on. Point out that the bread holds the sandwich together, just like the topic sentence and closing sentence hold together a paragraph. The meat, cheese, lettuce, and tomato inside are the "details" that fill the sandwich. Each piece builds upon the other.

2. Give students a copy of the **"A Space Pioneer"** and **Build It! Paragraph Chart reproducibles (pages 56–57)**. Use the chart to work as a class to put together the sentences from "A Space Pioneer" reproducible.

3. Remind students that a paragraph has structure. It has a topic sentence that usually states the main idea, supporting details that support the main idea, and a closing sentence that either transitions into the next paragraph or sums up the main idea. Details should be written in logical order. Tell students that they will work as a class to rearrange the sentences from "A Space Pioneer" in logical order. Work from a transparency of the Build It! reproducible.

4. Point out that the opening sentence usually presents the main idea that will be expanded on in the body of the paragraph. Ask students: *Which of these sentences best states what the paragraph will be about?* Write the answer in the top slice of bread: *Werner von Braun was a pioneer in the United States space program.*

5. Explain that the layers of the sandwich will include facts, examples, and other details that support or explain the main idea. Instruct students to look for clues to put them in the correct order. Ask: *Which is the earliest date you see? The latest date? When did von Braun move to the United States?* Write the supporting sentences in order in the middle layers of the sandwich.

6. The closing sentence should summarize or reinforce the main idea in the topic sentence. Look at the remaining sentence and ask: *Does this make a good closing sentence? Why?* If students agree that it does, write it in the bottom slice of bread. Invite a volunteer to read aloud the completed paragraph.

7. Explain that the paragraph you worked on together is called an expository paragraph, or a paragraph that defines or gives facts about a topic. Explain that a narrative paragraph tells a story.

8. Next, ask students to use the paragraph structure chart to write a narrative paragraph. Topics could include any event or topic of interest from their own lives, including *my favorite pet*, *my first dance*, or *my most embarrassing moment*.

9. Ask volunteers to share their paragraphs in small groups. Have group members decide if the topic sentence and closing sentence are effective and if the sentences are written in logical order.

Extended Learning

- Provide students with enlarged paragraphs cut from newspapers and magazines. Cut apart the sentences and place each paragraph in a separate plastic bag. Invite students to use the paragraph structure chart to reorder the sentences: topic sentence, supporting details, and closing sentence.

- Discuss the three main types of paragraphs: expository, narrative, and persuasive. Ask students to bring in samples of different kinds of paragraphs. Have them determine the kind of paragraph and discuss the strengths or weaknesses of the opening, supporting, and closing sentences.

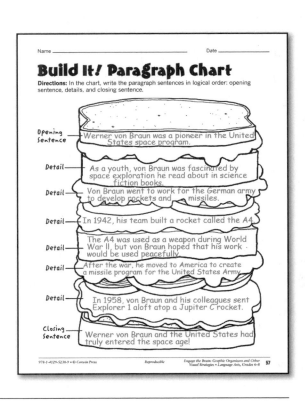

Name _____ Date _____

Build It! Paragraph Chart

Directions: In the chart, write the paragraph sentences in logical order: opening sentence, details, and closing sentence.

Opening Sentence — Werner von Braun was a pioneer in the United States space program.

Detail — As a youth, von Braun was fascinated by space exploration he read about in science fiction books.

Detail — Von Braun went to work for the German army to develop rockets and missiles.

Detail — In 1942, his team built a rocket called the A4.

Detail — The A4 was used as a weapon during World War II, but von Braun hoped that his work would be used peacefully.

Detail — After the war, he moved to America to create a missile program for the United States Army.

Detail — In 1958, von Braun and his colleagues sent Explorer 1 aloft atop a Jupiter C rocket.

Closing Sentence — Werner von Braun and the United States had truly entered the space age!

978-1-4129-5230-9 • © Corwin Press   Reproducible   *Engage the Brain: Graphic Organizers and Other Visual Strategies • Language Arts, Grades 6–8*   **57**

A Space Pioneer

In 1942, his team built a rocket called the *A4*.

Werner von Braun and the United States had truly entered the space age!

The *A4* was used as a weapon during World War II, but von Braun hoped that his work would be used peacefully.

Von Braun went to work for the German army to develop rockets and missiles.

In 1958, von Braun and his colleagues sent *Explorer 1* aloft atop a *Jupiter C* rocket.

Werner von Braun was a pioneer in the United States space program.

As a youth, von Braun was fascinated by space exploration he read about in science fiction books.

After the war, he moved to America to create a missile program for the United States Army.

Build It! Paragraph Chart

Directions: In the chart, write the paragraph sentences in logical order: opening sentence, details, and closing sentence.

Opening
Sentence

Detail

Detail

Detail

Detail

Detail

Detail

Closing
Sentence

Visual Poetry: Poetry Grids

Materials

Cinquain Poetry Grid reproducible

Diamante Poetry Grid reproducible

sample diamante and cinquain poems (from books or the Internet)

thesauruses, dictionaries

Tree

Lofty, lush

Soaring, whispering, swaying

The earth's evergreen offspring

Pine

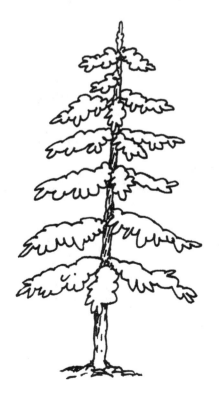

Skills Objectives

Use vivid, interesting adjectives.

Analyze word usage.

Recognize parts of speech.

Apply poetic form.

There is no doubt that writing poetry helps students in other areas of language arts. The diamante and cinquain are two forms of poetry that are particularly useful in vocabulary development. They also reinforce a student's understanding of parts of speech, emphasizing the connection between word study and writing. **Poetry Grids** can simplify the process of writing diamantes and cinquains, even for your most reluctant poets.

1. Begin by sharing examples of diamante and cinquain poems with students. Access the Internet to find different examples, or read from poetry books. Point out that these poems are not freeform but have a specific format.

2. Give students a copy of the **Cinquain Poetry Grid reproducible (page 60)**. Model the form of a cinquain on the board. Ask students to suggest a noun, or subject, for the poem, such as *tree*. Follow the form to complete the poem with students, using their suggestions for nouns, adjectives, and verbs.

Cinquain

Line 1: One word (noun) that names the subject of the poem (two syllables)

Line 2: Two words (adjectives) that describe the subject (two to four syllables)

Line 3: Three words (verbs) that describe something the subject does (six syllables)

Line 4: Four to six words that further describe or tell a feeling about the subject, often a complete sentence (eight syllables)

Line 5: One word that restates the subject of the poem (two syllables)

---

3. Next, give students a copy of the **Diamante Poetry Grid reproducible (page 61)**. Model the form of a diamante poem on the board. Invite students to help you choose a noun for the topic, such as *dog*. Point out that it's important to think about the two contrasting nouns that come at the beginning and end to make sure they will work. Use students' suggestions for nouns, adjectives, and gerunds.

> **Diamante**
> **Line 1:** One word (noun), subject A
> **Line 2:** Two words (adjectives) that describe subject A
> **Line 3:** Three gerunds (action verbs) that describe something subject A does
> **Line 4:** Four words (nouns)—two relate to subject A, and two relate to subject B
> **Line 5:** Three gerunds (action verbs) that describe something subject B does
> **Line 6:** Two words (adjectives) that describe subject B
> **Line 7:** One word (noun), subject B (must contrast with subject A, often an antonym)

4. Before having students write their own poems, make sure they understand each form of poetry. Allow them some leeway with syllables so they have more available word choices. Provide access to a thesaurus and a dictionary to help students find a variety of interesting, vivid words. Remind them to use brainstorming strategies such as clustering when choosing words.

Dog

Loyal, loving

Barking, playing, slurping

Chasing a ball, taking a nap

Grooming, purring, nuzzling

Elegant, graceful

Cat

Extended Learning

- Divide the class into groups, and have each group learn about a different form of poetry. Invite groups to share what they learned with the class.

- Help students publish their poetry in the school newspaper or newsletter. Contests and publishing opportunities are also available on the Internet:
    - Kids Bookshelf: *www.kidsbookshelf.com*
    - The Scholastic Art & Writing Awards: *www.scholastic.com/artandwritingawards/index.htm*
    - Amazing Kids' Amazing Writer's Library: *www.amazing-kids.org/writers.htm#top*

Cinquain Poetry Grid

Directions: Follow this format to write your own cinquain poem.

Line 1: One word (noun) that names the subject of the poem (two syllables)

Line 2: Two words (adjectives) that describe the subject (two to four syllables)

Line 3: Three words (verbs) that describe something the subject does (six syllables)

Line 4: Four to six words that further describe or tell a feeling about the subject, often a complete sentence (eight syllables)

Line 5: One word that restates the subject of the poem (two syllables)

Diamante Poetry Grid

Directions: Follow this format to write your own diamante poem.

Line 1: One word (noun), subject A

Line 2: Two words (adjectives) that describe subject A

Line 3: Three gerunds (action verbs) that describe something subject A does

Line 4: Four words (nouns), two relate to subject A, and two relate to subject B

Line 5: Three gerunds (action verbs) that describe something subject B does

Line 6: Two words (adjectives) that describe subject B

Line 7: One word (noun), subject B (must contrast with subject A, often an antonym)

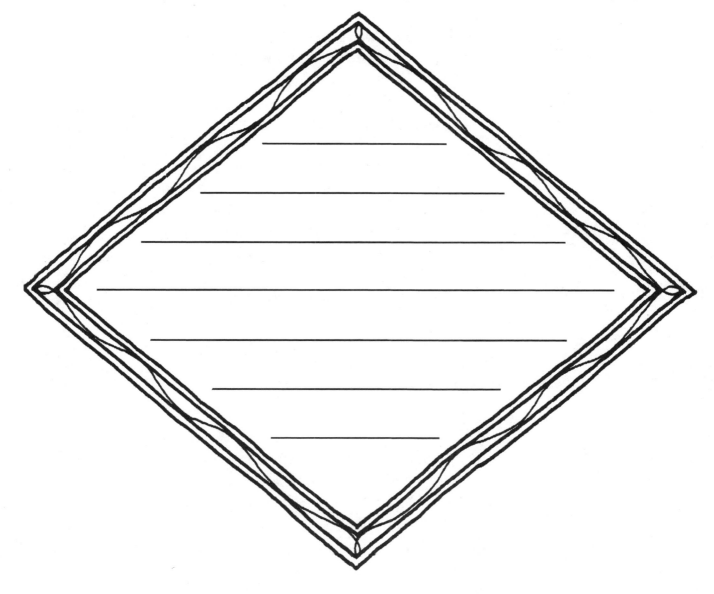

CHAPTER 3

Language Conventions

Right on Target: Word Web

<table>
<tr><td>

Materials

Right on Target reproducible

overhead projector and transparency (optional)

</td></tr>
</table>

Skills Objectives

Use interesting, specific adjectives.

Understand and use figurative language.

Word Webs are the workhorses of graphic organizers. They are visual maps used to gather and connect facts, ideas, and concepts. Webs provide a flexible framework for organizing information, and they show how words relate to each other. A word web is also a handy pre-reading or post-reading tool for developing vocabulary or working with descriptive and figurative language, including similes.

The goal of this extended word web activity is to begin with an object, use descriptive adjectives to describe the object, and finally, turn the adjectives into similes.

1. Ask students to define a simile. Accept any definition close to the following: *A comparison between two different things using the words **like** or **as**, designed to create a visual or emotional image.* Ask students for examples such as: *She is quiet as a mouse. The angry man roared like a lion. The breeze whispered as though it was telling a secret. The muffin was hard as a rock.*

2. Give students a copy of the **Right on Target reproducible (page 64)**. Draw an identical word web on the board, or place a transparency of the reproducible on the overhead. Write a noun in the center circle, such as *lake*.

3. With students, brainstorm adjectives to describe a lake. Examples include *blue, deep, smooth, cold, peaceful, misty, quiet, glassy,* and *lonely.* Choose six adjectives and write them in the middle sections around the web.

4. Add the word *like* or *as* after each adjective, and encourage students to think of nouns to complete a simile. Examples include *blue as the sky, peaceful like a sunset,* and *smooth as glass.* Choose two for each adjective and write them in the outer section of the web.

5. Once students feel comfortable with the process, instruct them to complete their own word webs using a noun of their choice. Make

sure students understand how to build a simile with an adjective. The simile should compare the word to something that provides a vivid image or idea.

6. When students are done with their webs, ask volunteers to share their similes with the class. Invite the class to vote on the most creative, vivid, interesting, and unusual similes.

Sample Similes

cold as ice	cute as a button	smooth as glass
easy as pie	sly like a fox	cry like a baby
light as a feather	dry as a bone	fits like a glove
quick as a wink	solid as a rock	fight like cats and dogs
smooth as silk	stiff as a board	laugh like a hyena
fresh as a daisy	straight like an arrow	slow as a snail
shy as a mouse	stubborn like a mule	sing like a bird
cool as a cucumber	tough as nails	sparkle like diamonds
big as an elephant	sweet as honey	work like a dog
brave as a lion	tight as a drum	snug as a bug in a rug
bright as day	thin as a rail	gentle as a lamb
busy as a bee	white as snow	mad as a hornet
clear as a bell	wise like an owl	slippery like an eel
proud as a peacock	eats like a bird	pretty as a picture
sharp as a knife	hungry as a bear	plain as day
clean as a whistle	flat as a pancake	silly as a goose

Extended Learning

- During independent reading time, have students collect similes, record them in a journal for future reference, and share them with the class.

- Have students illustrate common similes such as *cute as a button* or *free as a bird*.

- Write common similes, such as those listed above, on sentence strips for students. Cut the strips in half to make two sets. For example, one half would read *Flat as*, and the other half would read *a pancake*. Divide the class into two groups. Distribute one set of strips to each group, and then invite students to complete the similes by finding their matching half.

Right on Target

Directions: Write a noun in the center of the web. Write one adjective that describes the noun in each middle section of the web. In each outer section, write a simile using the noun and the adjective. Remember, a simile is a comparison between two objects using the words *like* or *as*.

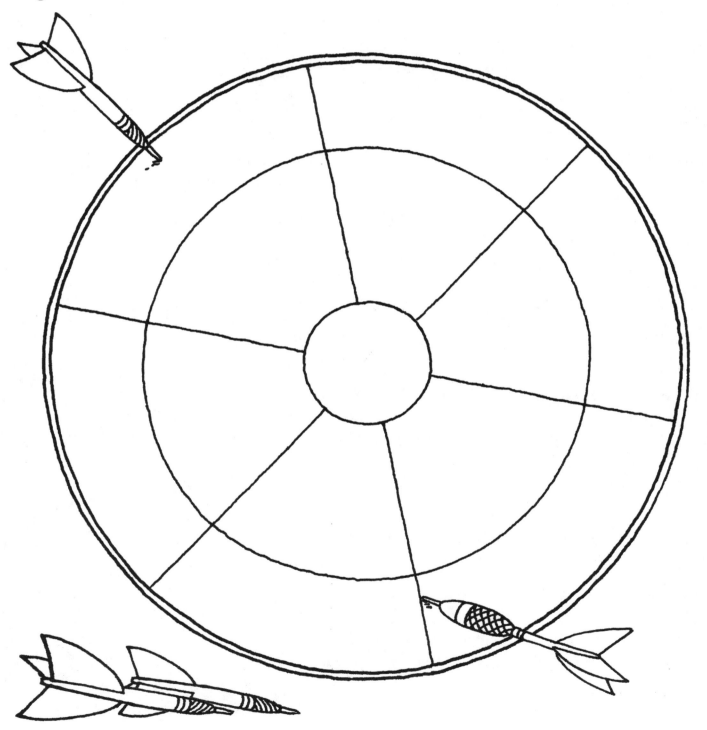

Lavish Language: Cluster Map

Skills Objectives
Recognize verb connotations.
Use precise language.

Materials
Lavish Language reproducible

overhead projector and transparency (optional)

thesauruses

An excellent strategy for improving student writing is to encourage the use of precise word choices. Vivid verbs and interesting adjectives can bring a sentence to life! Clustering helps young writers come up with many different options for the same action or description. Using a **Cluster Map** as a brainstorming tool encourages students to experiment with a variety of word meanings and connotations. Having a wide range of word choices will enhance students' writing by making the ordinary extraordinary.

1. Explain to the class that you will be using a simple cluster map to work on word connotation, the image that a word conveys. Write on the board: *Eric ate his lunch.* Below that sentence write: *Eric devoured his lunch* and *Eric nibbled his lunch.* Ask students: *What sort of image does each sentence bring to mind? Which sentence shows that Eric was very hungry? Which sentence shows that he wasn't very hungry?* Allow students time to respond. Invite them to think of other verbs that might convey a slightly different meaning, such as *dined, feasted, gobbled,* or *inhaled.*

2. Give students a copy of the **Lavish Language reproducible (page 67)**. Tell them that when they are writing, a cluster map can help them to brainstorm stronger, more vivid word choices.

3. Model using a cluster map on the board, or place a transparency of the reproducible on the overhead. In the center circle, write a simple verb such as *walk*. Ask students: *Does the word **walk** give you a strong image?* Invite students to think of five verbs that are more precise than *walk*, and write them in the next ring of circles. Some examples include: *saunter, stroll, march, rush, stagger, limp, tiptoe, strut,* and *prance.* Discuss the connotation of each new word.

4. Explain that using adverbs may refine the images even further. Select a verb such as *march*. Ask students: **How** did the person march? Students might answer: *slowly, proudly, happily,* or *angrily*. Write two adverbs in the circles connected to *march*.

5. Under your cluster map, write three sentences: *Ashley walked into the room. Ashley marched into the room. Ashley marched angrily into the room.* Discuss with students how each sentence becomes more defined in its meaning. Remind the class that overuse of adverbs can actually weaken writing, so it is important to choose the adverb that best reflects the image they want to convey.

6. Divide the class into small groups, and give each group a thesaurus. Assign each group a simple verb such as: *run, drink, hide, sleep, sit, said,* and *look*. Instruct students to work together to fill in their cluster maps. Before they begin, make sure they understand how to complete their maps correctly and follow the example on the board.

7. Once the cluster maps are complete, invite students to work independently to write five sentences using the verbs and adverbs they wrote. Allow volunteers to share their work with the class, and then discuss the image each sentence conveys.

Extended Learning

- Have students act out vivid verbs. For example, tell one student to walk across the front of the room. Next, ask a student to saunter, stroll, march, rush, stagger, limp, tiptoe, strut, and prance. Add adverbs to one or two verbs to strengthen the image, such as *limp slightly* or *limp painfully*.

- Have students use the cluster map to experiment with vivid nouns and adjectives. For instance, a *red book* could become a *crimson volume*. An *old house* could become an *ancient mansion*.

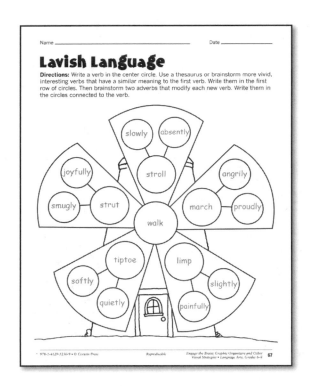

Lavish Language

Directions: Write a verb in the center circle. Use a thesaurus or brainstorm to come up with more vivid, interesting verbs that have a similar meaning to the first verb. Write them in the first ring of circles. Then brainstorm two adverbs that modify each new verb. Write them in the circles connected to the verb.

Up We Go! Ladder Organizer

Materials

Making Connections reproducible

Up We Go! reproducible

Skills Objectives

Build fluency.

Use a variety of organizational structures.

A ladder helps a person get from one place to another. In language, transitions do the same. They build a bridge between ideas and contribute to sentence fluency and text flow. A **Ladder Organizer** can serve several roles, including helping students choose appropriate transitions in their writing. Using effective transitions can help students employ a variety of sentence lengths that result in a more rhythmic and fluid writing style.

1. Review with students what they already know about using transitions. Explain that transitional words and phrases clarify or link ideas, helping one idea flow to the next. Read the following two sentences aloud: *Mia studied hard. She didn't do very well on the test.* Then read aloud these two sentences: *Mia studied hard. However, she didn't do very well on the test.* Ask students which sentence pair sounds better. Point out that second pair flowed better because the word *however* led them to the second idea.

2. Write a selection of transitions on the board. Use the samples from the following list or choose your own. Explain that transitional words have different meanings or connotations. Before using a particular transition, be sure you understand its meaning and usage. Transitions can be used to link two sentences together or begin a new sentence to connect one idea to the next. Ask students: *Which of these words would you use to contrast two ideas?* (but) Invite a couple of volunteers to use the word *but* in a sentence, for example: *Josh wanted to go to the park, but it was raining.*

> **Sample Transitions**
>
> **Addition, Sequence:** moreover, furthermore, in addition, also, incidentally, by the way, further, too, again, more important, next, first, second, et cetera, last, finally, either, as well
>
> **Contrast:** however, yet, in contrast on the other hand, in any case, on the contrary, still, otherwise, actually, all the same, at any rate, at the same time, nevertheless, instead, in spite of this, anyway, by contrast
>
> **Comparison:** likewise, similarly, in the same way, in like manner, whereas

> **Cause, Result, Purpose:** therefore, thus, hence, consequently, after all, to be sure, for this reason, accordingly, then, knowing this, naturally, of course, with this object, to this end, because of this, with this in mind, in many cases, in this way, as
>
> **Example, Restatement, Conclusion:** for example, for instance, more specifically, in particular, indeed, in other words, in fact, that is, in brief, in short, to summarize, in conclusion
>
> **Time:** afterwards, later on, soon, meanwhile, in the meantime, next, immediately, then, later, at length, eventually, at the same time, in the same instant, today, nowadays, in the beginning, to begin, in time, in future, finally, initially
>
> **Place:** here, there, nearby, beyond, further on, opposite, on the opposite side, on the right, on the left, behind, in back

3. Give each student one copy of the **Making Connections reproducible (page 70)** and two copies of the **Up We Go! reproducible (page 71)**. Model the first pair of sentences with the class. Read them aloud; write the first sentence in the space below the first rung of the ladder; and write the second sentence in the space above.

4. Ask students: *What transitional word would best connect these two sentences? Might it tell **when** Bill paid for the soda?* Several sequence words would work, such as *then* and *before*. Write your new sentence on the board: *Bill paid for the soda before he drank it.* Have students write sentences on a separate sheet of paper.

5. Tell students to work their way up the ladder by joining the remaining sentence pairs. Remind students to think carefully to determine which transition fits logically with each sentence pair.

6. When students are done joining all the sentences, invite pairs to check each other's work. Have them discuss if the transitions fit correctly and help ideas flow from one to the next.

Extended Learning

- Ask students to go "fishing" for transitional words and phrases in newspapers and magazines. Have them highlight any they find and bring them to class.

- Discuss how transitional words can change the meaning of a sentence, such as: *Jackie loves the city because of the crowds,* or *Jackie loves the city in spite of the crowds.*

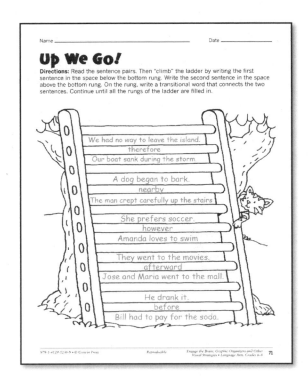

Making Connections

Directions: Use the Up We Go! ladder organizer to help you join these sentence pairs using transitions.

1. Bill had to pay for the soda.
   He drank it.

2. Jose and Marie went to the mall.
   They went to the movies.

3. Amanda loves to swim.
   She prefers soccer.

4. The man crept carefully up the stairs.
   A dog began to bark.

5. Our boat sank during the storm.
   We had no way to leave the island.

6. Everyone had fun at the party.
   It went on late into the evening.

7. The rain poured down on the hikers.
   They continued up the trail to the mountaintop.

8. Lauren is interested in studying law.
   She is applying to several law schools across the country.

9. Trey broke his bike during the race.
   He wasn't able to cross the finish line.

10. Some chemicals have a strong reaction when mixed together.
    If you put baking soda into a glass of vinegar, it will create lots of foam.

Up We Go!

Directions: Read the sentence pairs. Then "climb" the ladder by writing the first sentence in the space below the bottom rung. Write the second sentence in the space above the bottom rung. On the rung, write a transitional word that connects the two sentences. Continue until all the rungs of the ladder are filled in.

Branching Out: Network Tree Organizer

Materials

Branching Out reproducible

overhead projector

2 transparencies

dictionaries, thesauruses

Skills Objectives

Apply prior knowledge.

Understand elements of word building.

Build new words using prefixes and suffixes.

Network Tree Organizers are hierarchical graphic organizers. Students can use them to sort and classify information and show how elements are related. One possible application is to show prefixes, suffixes, and the words they are used to build. Understanding prefixes and suffixes builds skills in spelling and vocabulary and improves reading comprehension. Prefixes and suffixes are effective clues for helping students decipher unfamiliar words.

1. Write several words, such as *telephone, telescope,* and *television,* on the board. Ask what these words have in common. *(the prefix **tele-**)* Ask students how this prefix helps them figure out the word meanings. Then explain: **Tele-** *means distant. We can talk to someone far away on a telephone; we can see faraway stars through a telescope; and we can see faraway pictures on television.*

2. Inform students that you will be working together on word-building skills. Ask them to define the meaning of *prefix* and *suffix. (They are word parts that contribute to or change the meaning of words.)* Learning common prefixes and suffixes will help students guess the meaning of unfamiliar words.

3. Brainstorm with students a selection of prefixes and suffixes. Write responses on the board, including the meanings.

Prefixes	Meaning	Sample Words
auto–	self	automobile, automatic
circu–	around	circumference, circulate
dec–	ten	decade, decathlon
equi–	equal	equilateral, equation
inter–	between	interactive, international
micro–	small	microscope, microwave
mid–	middle	midnight, midway
mono–	one	monogamy, monarch
sub–	under, below	submarine, subzero
trans–	across	transfer, translate

4. Give students a copy of the **Branching Out reproducible (page 74)**. Draw two sample network trees on the board, or place two

transparencies of the reproducible on the overhead. Write *Prefix* in the bottom circle of Tree #1 and *Suffix* in the bottom circle of Tree #2. Then, in the first row of circles on Tree #1, write five prefixes. Review the definition of each prefix with the class. Then ask students to suggest two sample words for each prefix, and write them in the two connecting circles. Repeat the activity using suffixes on Tree #2.

Suffixes	Meaning	Sample Words
–al	relating to	sensual, natural
–dom	state or quality of	freedom, boredom
–cule	very small	molecule, miniscule
–ee	one who receives the action	employee, nominee
–ful	full of	beautiful, helpful
–ify	to make	satisfy, terrify
–ist	one who does something	biologist, artist
–ly	like	clearly, fearlessly
–ology	study of	geology, anthropology
–ward	direction	eastward, westward

5. Have students work with partners to complete two network tree organizers, one for prefixes and one for suffixes. Check with each pair to make sure they understand the assignment. Have dictionaries and thesauruses available.

6. Invite students to work independently to write a sentence for each of the ten sample words in the last row of their network tree organizer.

Extended Learning

- Ask students to read a passage in a newspaper or magazine and use a highlighter to mark words that incorporate prefixes or suffixes.

- Explain that many prefixes and suffixes have Greek or Latin roots. Ask students to use a computer or dictionary to find the origins of common prefixes and suffixes.

- Initiate a class discussion on root words. Explain that the root is the base of a word before prefixes or suffixes are added. For example, in the word *unreadable*, *read* is the root word, the core meaning. Select a root word and invite students to help you make as many new words as possible.

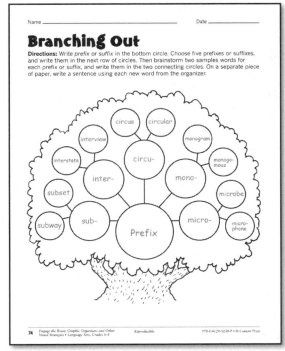

Branching Out

Directions: Write *prefix* or *suffix* in the bottom circle. Choose five prefixes or suffixes, and write them in the next row of circles. Then brainstorm two samples words for each prefix or suffix, and write them in the two connecting circles. On a separate piece of paper, write a sentence using each new word from the organizer.

Vivid Vocabulary: Word Wheel

Skills Objectives
Demonstrate effective use of adjectives.
Choose precise language.
Use dictionary and thesaurus skills.

Materials
Vivid Vocabulary reproducible

red object (e.g., apple or scarf)

dictionaries, thesauruses

Synonyms and antonyms are often presented as lists. An organizer such as a **Word Wheel** allows students to present them visually in related groupings. Understanding the subtle differences between synonyms or antonyms helps students choose precise words for more vivid, interesting writing. In addition, identifying the nuances between various synonyms and antonyms is an excellent way to build vocabulary skills.

1. In front of the class, hold up something red, such as an apple or scarf. Ask them what color it is. You will most likely hear the word *red*. Ask students: *What other words might you use to describe the color of this object? What is another word for **red**?* You might get answers such as: *burgundy, cardinal, cherry, crimson, garnet, rose, ruby, ruddy,* or *scarlet*.

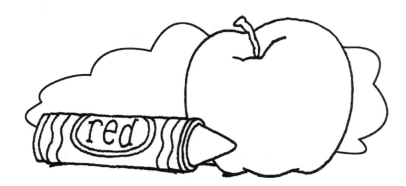

2. Then ask students if your question was easy. *What is the opposite of **easy**?* Answers might include: *difficult, hard, challenging, arduous, tough, rough,* or *trying*.

3. Explain that the words *red* and *easy* are adjectives, words used to describe something. Point out that using a precise adjective instead of a commonplace or overused adjective can make writing more vivid, interesting, and specific. With students, brainstorm overused adjectives such as *happy, sad, big, little, tall, short, mad, hot, cold,* and so on. Point out how specific words can improve a sentence. For example, *I ate a big piece of good chocolate cake* sounds much better as *I devoured a colossal chunk of scrumptious chocolate cake.*

4. Give students a copy of the **Vivid Vocabulary reproducible (page 77)**. Then draw a sample word wheel on the board. Point out the circle at the center of the wheel, like a bull's-eye.

5. Invite students to suggest simple "target adjectives" to write in the circle, such as *sad*. Then ask them to brainstorm synonyms for *sad*. Write the synonyms in the middle section between the spokes of the wheel: *blue, gloomy, glum, sorrowful, forlorn, down, depressed, cheerless*. Repeat the process, but this time, have students suggest antonyms for *sad*, such as *happy, cheerful, glad, gleeful, upbeat, merry, jolly, joyous*. Write these words in the outer sections of the wheel.

6. Divide the class into small groups. Make sure they know how to use the word wheel. Assist as needed.

7. Give each group a target adjective to write in the center of their wheel. Allow groups ten minutes to fill in their word wheels with a list of synonyms and antonyms for their adjective. Provide access to thesauruses and dictionaries. Suggest that students use different colored pens to write synonyms and antonyms.

8. When groups are finished, have them share their words with the class. Invite volunteers to think of and write sentences using the new words. Point out how the new words create vivid imagery and more exciting writing.

Extended Learning

- To further illustrate vivid writing, include a noun with the target word, such as *hot sun*. Have students fill in synonyms for *hot*: *burning, steamy, fiery, sweltering, blazing, roasting, blistering, flaming*. Ask volunteers to suggest sentences using the words. For example: *I felt the burning sun (steamy sun, fiery sun, sweltering sun, blazing sun, roasting sun, blistering sun, flaming sun) on my skin.* Have the class choose the adjective that works best.

- With students, play a game based on the popular game *Password*™. Whisper a target word to one student. That student gives clues in the form of synonyms to a partner, who must guess the target word.

Name _____ Date _____

Vivid Vocabulary

Directions: Write a word in the center of the word wheel. Then write synonyms for the word in the middle sections and antonyms in the outer sections.

joyous · happy · cheerful · glad · gleeful · upbeat · merry · jolly

blue · gloomy · glum · sorrowful · forlorn · down · depressed · cheerless

sad

Vivid Vocabulary

Directions: Write a word in the center of the word wheel. Then write synonyms for the word in the middle sections and antonyms in the outer sections.

CHAPTER 4

Listening and Speaking

The Art of Listening: KWL Chart

Materials

"Medusa"
reproducible

Art of Listening
reproducible

nonfiction passages

Skills Objectives

Read for a purpose.
Use prior knowledge.
Identify relevant details and key information.
Practice good listening skills.

Active listening incorporates a number of skills, most important, understanding, analyzing, and anticipating information. As a pre-listening activity, the **KWL Chart** prepares students by having them draw on previous knowledge, anticipate what will come, target particular information, and summarize what they learned. The chart can also be used as a study guide or a source for a report outline.

1. Tell two students to carry on a conversation while you read aloud a passage of text. When you're finished reading, ask the class if they had difficulty listening to you read or if they were distracted.

2. Ask students: *What do you think **active listening** means? What do you think someone needs to do to be an active listener?* You may get a wide variety of responses, such as: *Sit close to the speaker; look at the speaker; ignore distractions; lean forward;* and so on. Guide the discussion toward another idea: *Read about the subject ahead of time.*

3. Give students a copy of the **Art of Listening reproducible (page 81)**. Draw an identical chart on the board to work on as a class. Explain that the *K* stands for what they already *know*. The *W* stands for what they *want* to learn. The *L* stands for what they *learn*.

4. Inform students that you are going to read aloud a story about a mythological being named Medusa. Use the **"Medusa" reproducible (page 80)**.

5. Before reading, encourage students to brainstorm what they already know about Medusa. Answers might include: *She had snakes for hair. She turned people to stone.* Next, have them think of what they want to learn about her, such as: *How did she turn into a monster? Where did she live?* Write student responses on the class KWL chart.

6. Read aloud the story about Medusa. While you read, tell students to listen carefully and take notes, particularly when they hear a fact noted in the *W* column of the chart.

7. After you read the story, ask students: *Did you confirm what you already knew about Medusa? Did you learn what you wanted to know?* Invite students to offer new facts for the *L* column that they learned from the reading.

8. Choose another selection from a nonfiction book or an article from a magazine or encyclopedia, and repeat the activity. This time, have students work independently to fill in their KWL charts.

9. Once the activity is complete, ask students if they felt more engaged in the listening process by using the chart. Discuss other ways that students can be more active listeners.

Extended Learning

• Tape-record a news program about a topical issue. Give students the topic covered in the story, and have them fill out a KWL chart before listening to the tape. Then play the tape, and have them finish their charts.

• Initiate a discussion about clue words. Explain that when someone is speaking or lecturing, they use clues to signal that important information will follow, such as: *also, in addition, most important, specifically,* and *especially.* Ask students to suggest clue words that might be used when a speaker is summarizing. Answers might include: *in conclusion, for this reason,* and *finally.* How about when a speaker is trying to show cause and effect? Word clues might include: *because, consequently,* and *therefore.*

• People also use physical clues called *body language* when they speak. Discuss the meaning of certain types of body language. Ask students: *When two people are having a conversation, what does their body language tell you? What if one person is leaning forward and the other is leaning back? What if one is looking forward and the other is looking away or looking down?*

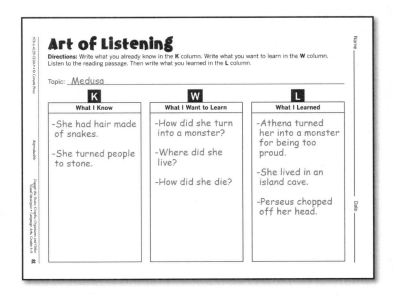

Medusa

Have you ever heard someone say they were "scared stiff"? That was certainly true of anyone who saw a gorgon! There were three gorgons, and they were sisters. These sisters were so hideous that just one glance turned the victim to stone. The best known of the three was Medusa, but she had not always been ugly. In fact, it was her beauty that caused her terrible fate.

Medusa was once incredibly beautiful, particularly her long, gleaming hair. The sea god, Poseidon, was in love with her. Although she was beautiful, Medusa wasn't very wise. She bragged about her beauty and claimed she was even more beautiful than the goddess Athena. This was a huge mistake. When Athena heard about Medusa's claim, she turned the conceited girl into a monster. Medusa's magnificent hair was turned into a mass of wriggling, slithering snakes.

Medusa hid in an island cave to plot her revenge. She turned any living creature who dared to look upon her to stone. The stone bodies of these unfortunate souls littered the entrance to her hidden cave. Medusa had transformed them into lifeless statues, frozen in terror. No one was brave enough to face her except a young hero named Perseus. Athena provided Perseus with a polished shield and a razor-sharp sword. When the wise young man finally found the hidden gorgon monster, he looked not at her face, but at her reflection in his shield. With one great swoop, he cut off her head!

At her death, a few drops of Medusa's blood fell into the sea. In memory of the beautiful woman he once knew, Poseidon mixed the blood with the pounding waves. From this frothy sea foam was born one of the most magnificent of magical beasts: the snow-white, winged stallion, Pegasus.

Art of Listening

Directions: Write what you already know in the **K** column. Write what you want to learn in the **W** column. Listen to the reading passage. Then write what you learned in the **L** column.

Topic: _____

K What I Know	**W** What I Want to Learn	**L** What I Learned

In the Headlines: 5W Chart

Materials

"Honor for Loyal Fan" reproducible

In the Headlines reproducible

newspaper articles

Skills Objectives

Listen for information.
Practice good listening skills.
Record facts accurately from a verbal source.

Newspapers have always been an important tool in the classroom. They generally offer a concise, tightly organized story with clear emphasis on facts. Using a **5W Chart** in conjunction with a newspaper encourages students to listen carefully as they note important facts and details. 5W charts also help students focus on the *who, when, where, what,* and *why* of nonfiction or news articles.

1. The day before you do this activity, ask students to bring a selection of newspaper articles to class, or bring in a couple of newspapers from which students can choose articles.

2. Explain that for newspaper articles as well as other nonfiction passages, students must answer five questions in order to get all the facts, the five W's. The five W's stand for *who, what, when, where,* and *why*. Write the words on the board.

3. Inform students that you will be reading aloud a short newspaper article, **"Honor for Loyal Fan" (page 84)**. As you read, they will listen carefully for the answers to the five W's. If they hear an answer, they should raise their hands. Reinforce the importance of good listening skills such as leaning forward, focusing on the speaker, no talking, and so on.

4. Begin reading the article aloud. As soon as you reach an answer to one of the five W's (*who*), pause and look up. Most students should have their hands raised. Invite a volunteer to share the information he or she heard. *(Minnie Davison)* Write the answer next to *who* on the board. Continue reading the article and writing answers next to the remaining questions, *what, when, where,* and *why*.

5. Give students a copy of the **In the Headlines reproducible (page 85)**. Tell students they will work with a partner to answer the five W's in a newspaper article. Allow student pairs to choose two articles to work with. Have partners take turns reading aloud an article and listening for the answers. Have them write the information in their charts. Before they begin, remind them how to be active listeners.

6. When students are done with the activity, discuss with the class whether they felt their articles were newsworthy. Ask: *Why or why not? What additional questions would you like answered about this story?*

Extended Learning

- Have students write a two- or three-sentence summary about the article they read and draw a picture to accompany it.

- Invite students to read a selection of newspaper letters to the editor. Ask them to write a letter to the editor commenting on one of the letters they read.

- The purpose of a newspaper headline is to grab your attention and make you want to read the article. Ask students to think of additional attention-grabbing, creative titles for their news articles.

Honor for Loyal Fan

NEWS

One of the fine citizens of Rochester hasn't missed a Rochester High football game in more than 50 years. Who is this loyal football fan? Minnie Davison of 442 Willow Street! Last Friday night the Rochester Lions thanked her for her support by dedicating their new field in her honor.

"I grew up going to football games with my father," Mrs. Davison claimed proudly. "He coached the Rochester Lions for 25 years. He would be so proud of this new field."

A plaque in Mrs. Davison's honor is at the entry gate of the field, and she was presented with a gold pendant in the shape of a lion.

"I don't know what I would do if I looked into the stands and she wasn't there," smiled Dominic Evangeli, current coach of the state champion football team. "She is our good luck charm."

Mrs. Davison accepted her honor at halftime on the 50-yard line of the football field. She was brought to tears when she received a standing ovation from the crowd.

Minnie Davison Proudly Accepts Plaque

When asked if there was anything else she was hoping for, she nodded. "I'd like our boys to make a couple more touchdowns."

Minnie got her wish. The Lions won the game with a score of 27 to 14.

In the Headlines

Directions: Listen carefully to the article. Write the headline. Then write *who* the article was about, *what* happened, *when* it happened, *where* it happened, and *why* it happened.

Daily Bugle

Headline	Who?
What?	When?
Where?	Why?

Speak Up! Persuasive Speech Map

Skills Objectives

Recognize the main idea.
Use facts to support the main idea.
Use persuasive language.
Practice presentation skills.

Materials

Speak Up! reproducible

overhead projector and transparency

Before giving a persuasive speech, students must consider what position they will take and how they can support their argument. A **Persuasive Speech Map** is designed to help students facilitate this kind of presentation by allowing them to record their position statement, reasons for their position, and supporting details and/or examples in one organized visual.

1. Engage students in a discussion about the qualities of a good class president. For example: *smart, responsible, friendly, mature, has good ideas to improve the school, good leadership skills*, and so on.

2. Tell students that they are going to give a three-minute persuasive speech. They can choose from two position statements: *Why I Should Be Class President* or *Why (Student of Choice) Should Be Class President.*

3. Give students a copy of the **Speak Up! reproducible (page 88)**, and place a transparency of the reproducible on the overhead. Show students how to write a position statement in the center oval.

4. Then brainstorm with students one reason they feel would convince their classmates to vote for a certain student, or themselves, for class president. Prompt students with questions such as: *Why would you make a good class president? Do you have any experience with leadership? What would you do if you were elected president? Would you change any school rules? Do you have something special to offer your school?* Write one reason in one branch of the map, such as: *Good leadership skills.*

5. Explain to students that a reason is not persuasive in itself. Reasons must be backed up with examples or supporting evidence. Point out the outer circles on the map. This is where students will provide examples to back up their reasons. Write a couple of examples that support good leadership skills, such as: *captain of the soccer team; coordinated school recycling project.*

6. Encourage students to complete the persuasive speech map individually. Check to make sure that they understand how to fill in the map, giving four reasons and at least two examples that support each reason. Remind students that their position statement should persuade others why either they or another student should be class president.

7. Once the organizers are complete, allow students to write their speeches as a homework assignment. Remind them that the point of the speech is to convince voters (classmates), so the language should be specific and persuasive. Set aside time for students to deliver their speeches. Allow the class to vote on which speech was the most persuasive and why.

Extended Learning

- Encourage students to create campaign posters they can display around the classroom.

- Point out that giving a speech is not just content, it's also presentation. With students, brainstorm good presentation skills, such as the following:
  - dress nicely and neatly
  - make eye contact with the audience
  - speak clearly and loudly enough to be heard and understood
  - don't rush the speech
  - emphasize important points
  - be confident

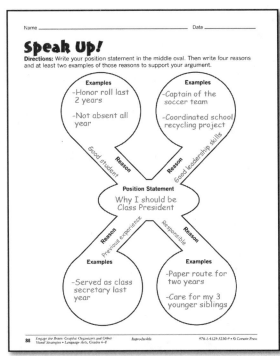

Name _____   Date _____

Speak Up!

Directions: Write your position statement in the middle oval. Then write four reasons and at least two examples of those reasons to support your argument.

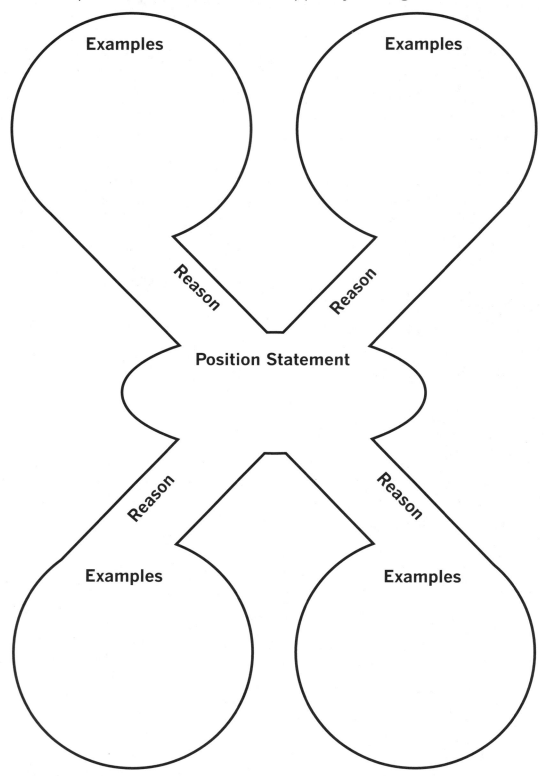

Examples

Examples

Reason

Reason

Position Statement

Reason

Reason

Examples

Examples

 Engage the Brain: Graphic Organizers and Other Visual Strategies • Language Arts, Grades 6–8   Reproducible   978-1-4129-5230-9 • © Corwin Press

Information Please: SQ3R Chart

Skills Objectives
Read for a purpose.
Use prior knowledge.
Practice presentation skills.

Materials
"The Moon" reproducible

SQ3R Chart reproducible

An **SQ3R Chart** helps students think actively while reading, particularly while reading for research purposes. SQ3R stands for **S**urvey, **Q**uestion, **R**ead, **R**ecite, and **R**eview. This chart guides students through a series of steps that incorporate prior knowledge and enhance comprehension and retention. Using an SQ3R chart is an excellent way for students to prepare for an exam or an oral report.

1. Give two copies of the **SQ3R Chart reproducible (page 92)** to each student. Explain that SQ3R is a reading strategy that will help them retain information. Break down each step for students.

> **Survey:** Skim the text first before reading. Look at the title, headings, captions, featured vocabulary, pictures, diagrams, and review questions to get a general idea of the content.
>
> **Question:** After surveying the text, think about the questions that came to mind. *What information would you like to learn from reading the material? What do you already know about the subject?*
>
> **Read:** Read the material. Find answers to your questions as you read. Reread parts that are unclear.
>
> **Recite:** Take notes from the text to summarize the information. Recite your notes aloud. Read aloud your questions and answers to reinforce learning.
>
> **Review:** Review your notes. Page through the text to review the important points. Make flashcards and create mnemonic devices to help you remember main ideas.

2. Tell students they will use this strategy and the accompanying chart to prepare and present a short oral report. Give them a copy of **"The Moon" reproducible (page 91)**. Demonstrate how to complete the chart using this passage.

3. Write on the board: *Survey, Question, Read, Recite,* and *Review.* Tell students: *Don't read the body of the text yet.* Guide them in a survey of the title, subject headings, featured vocabulary, and the diagram and captions. Ask: *What do you think the passage is*

about? Write responses on the board under *Survey*. Have students follow along on their SQ3R chart.

4. Next, read a subject heading and show students how to turn it into a question. For example, *Lunar Phases* can become *What are the phases of the moon?* Ask students: *Do you have any other questions about the text?* Write responses on the board under *Question*.

5. Read the full text, or have volunteers read each section aloud. Instruct the class to listen for the answers to their questions and write them on the chart under *Read*.

6. The *Recite* step will help commit the information to memory. Tell students they will read aloud what they have learned from the reading. Invite volunteers to read questions and answers from the SQ3R chart one at a time. Recopy the most important information in the *Recite* section, and read it aloud again.

7. In the final *Review* step, students get one more chance to review and take notes on the most important information. This is an overview of the key information they would use in an oral report. It is also a handy study guide for a test.

8. Instruct students to select a topic for an oral report, or invite them to report on current news events or a topic being studied in class. Have them use the SQ3R chart as a research tool to help build their reports. Make sure students understand the steps of the SQ3R method, and assist as needed.

9. Set aside time for students to present their reports. Remind students to speak slowly and clearly and use their SQ3R charts as a guide.

Extended Learning

- Bring in old newspapers and magazines. Have students find an article of interest and then fill in a SQ3R chart based on their chosen article. Tell them to use a highlighter to mark important points in the text.

- Have students use SQ3R charts as a review technique before a test.

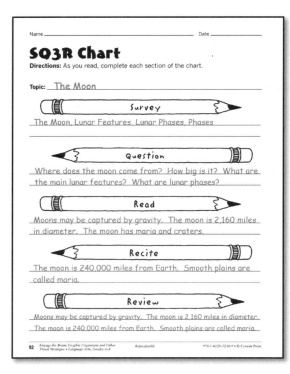

The Moon

A moon is a natural body, or **satellite**, that revolves around a planet. Moons have various origins. Some may have formed from materials left over after the planets formed. Some may be space objects captured in orbit by a planet's gravity. Others may be the remains of collisions between larger objects in space. All of the planets except Mercury and Venus have one or more moons. Earth has only one moon. At 2,160 miles in diameter, our moon is about one-quarter the size of Earth. The average distance of the moon from Earth is about 240,000 miles.

Lunar Features

Have you ever noticed during a full moon that you can see a "face" on the lunar surface? The moon's features are formed by dark, smooth plains called **maria** (*mare* if you're talking about just one). *Maria* is Latin for "seas." They formed millions and millions of years ago as molten rock flowed through cracks in the surface and hardened.

There are also thousands of meteorite **craters** on the moon. These craters were formed between three and four billion years ago, but they haven't changed much since then because the moon has no water or atmosphere to wear them away. The crater called Copernicus is easy to see from Earth with the naked eye. It is nearly 60 miles across.

Lunar Phases

It takes a little less than 30 days for the moon to rotate once on its axis and complete one **orbit** around Earth. Just like Earth, half of the lunar surface is always lit by the sun. But as the moon changes position in its orbit, an observer on Earth sees different amounts of the sunlit area. It almost looks like the moon is changing shape. Each shape is called a **phase**.

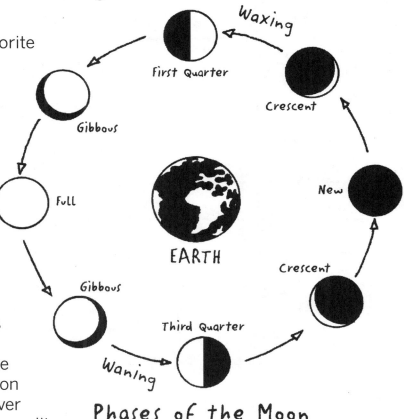

Phases of the Moon

SQ3R Chart

Directions: As you read, complete each section of the chart.

Topic: _____

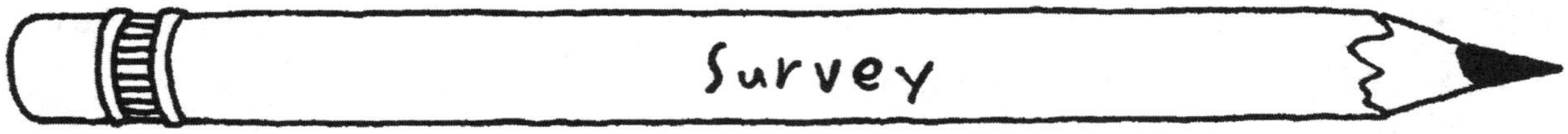

Survey

Question

Read

Recite

Review

It's Debatable: T-Chart

Skills Objectives
Compare and contrast information.
Distinguish between fact and opinion.
Express oral opinions about a topic.
Use persuasive language.
Practice presentation skills.

Materials
It's Debatable
reproducible

Classification charts such as a **T-Chart** enable students to list information about two elements and then visually compare, contrast, and clarify the material. Topics may be examined, such as: *pros and cons*, *advantages and disadvantages*, *cause and effect*, *problems and solutions*, *fact and opinion*, or *before and after*. A T-chart is handy for organizing information for an oral report; and because it shows different perspectives, it is an excellent tool for planning a debate strategy.

1. Ask students to raise their hands if they think the student body should be able to plan lunch menus in the cafeteria. Allow students to respond and give reasons for their answers. Then respond with reasons why students should *not* be able to choose the menu, such as: *They may choose unhealthy foods*; *it may be more expensive*; and so on. Explain that students have just participated in a debate.

2. Tell the class that they are going to participate in a short debate. Give each student two copies of the **It's Debatable reproducible (page 95)**. Then draw a simple T-chart on the board.

3. Explain that in a debate, one person forms an opinion about a topic and argues his or her point of view while another person takes the opposite side and argues his or her point of view. Give examples of topics such as: *Our school should have a dress code*, or *cell phones should not be allowed in school*.

4. Select a debate topic to demonstrate how to complete the chart. For example: *Students should be able to wear costumes to school on Halloween.* Write the topic above the chart. Ask students: *What are some reasons students should be allowed to wear Halloween costumes to school?* Write responses on the board in the *Yes/Pro* column. Then ask: *What are some reasons students should **not** wear costumes to school?* Write responses in the *No/Con* column.

5. Point out that during a debate each person has a chance to present information to support his or her case. Review what is written in the *Yes/Pro* column of the T-chart and ask: *Which of these points will support the **Yes** side?* Then review the *No/Con* column of the chart.

6. Explain that after both sides have made their points, they each get to try to disprove or discredit the points made by the opposing side. Tell them this is called a rebuttal. *To present a good rebuttal you have to know what points your opponents will probably use. That is why you complete both sides of the T-chart, to help you learn about both sides of the topic.*

7. After students have helped to complete your T-chart, ask them to suggest topics for a class debate. Divide the class into small teams, and give one topic to each pair of teams. Have teams complete their T-charts presenting both sides of the topic.

8. Then invite each pair of teams to debate their topic for the class. Allow the class to vote on which team presented the best case.

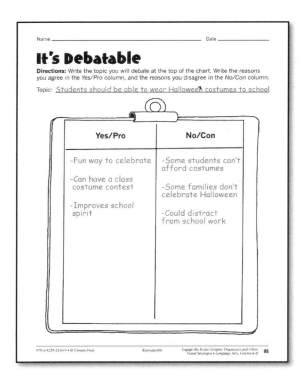

Extended Learning

- Explain that in a debate it is important to support points with facts rather than opinions. Have students bring in articles from magazines. Using a T-chart labeled *Fact* and *Opinion*, ask them to read an article and then write on the chart at least three facts and two opinions from the article.

- Another example of a classification chart is a Venn diagram. Have students complete a T-chart about the strengths and weaknesses of two books or movie characters. Then have them use the information to create a Venn diagram comparing the two characters. Tell students to compare the T-chart and the Venn diagram.

It's Debatable

Directions: Write the topic you will debate at the top of the chart. Write the reasons you agree in the *Yes/Pro* column, and the reasons you disagree in the *No/Con* column.

Topic: _____

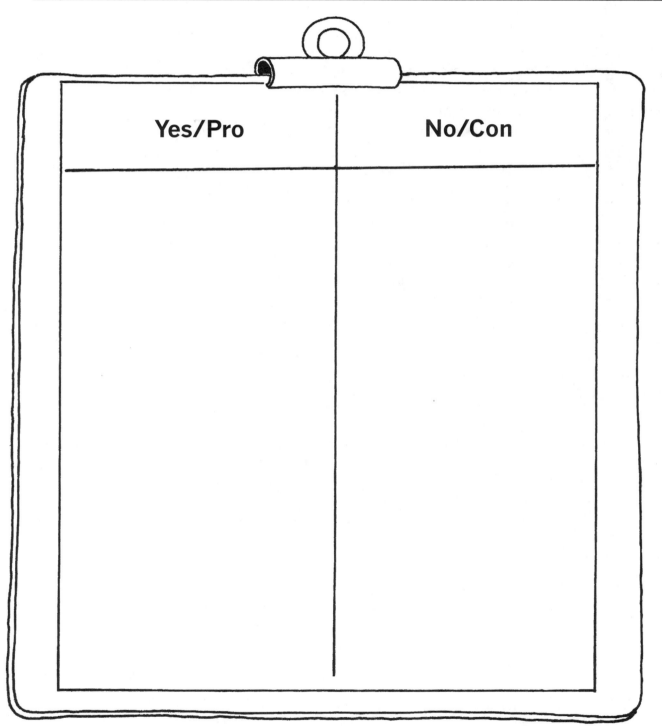

Yes/Pro	No/Con

References

Anderson, S. (Ed.). (1982). *Simon & Schuster's guide to mammals*. New York, NY: Simon & Schuster.

The Anne Frank Center USA Online. (n.d.). *Timeline*. Retrieved August 30, 2006, from http://www.annefrank. com/2_life_timeline_5.htm.

Baker, D. (1982). *The history of manned space flight*. New York, NY: New Cavendish Books.

Bromley, K., Irwin-De Vitis, L., & Modlo, M. (1995). *Graphic organizers: Visual strategies for active learning*. New York, NY: Scholastic Professional Books.

Byers, J. (2004). *Instructional strategies online: What are graphic organizers?* Retrieved August 15, 2006, from http://olc. spsd.sk.ca/DE/PD/instr/strats/graphicorganizers.

Couper, H., & Henbest, N. (1992). *The space atlas*. London, England: Dorling Kindersley.

Forte, I., & Schurr, S. (2001). *Standards-based language arts graphic organizers, rubrics, and writing prompts for middle grade students*. Nashville, TN: Incentive Publications, Inc.

Gardner, H. (1983). *Frames of mind: The theory of multiple intelligences*. New York, NY: Basic Books.

Golding, W. (1954). *The lord of the flies*. New York, NY: Berkley Publishing Group.

Graphic.org. (n.d.). *The graphic organizer*. Retrieved August 10, 2006, from http://www.graphic.org.

The Science Classroom at Mohave High School. (n.d.). *Graphic organizers*. Retrieved August 10, 2006, from http:// gotoscience.com/Graphic_Organizers.html#Toppage.

Hall, T., & Strangman, N. (2002). *Graphic organizers*. Retrieved August 15, 2006, from http://www.cast.org/ publications/ncac/ncac_go.html.

Hendricks, R. A. (1979). *Mythologies of the world: A concise encyclopedia*. New York, NY: McGraw-Hill.

Hopkins, G. (2003). *Debates in the classroom*. Retrieved September 20, 2006, from http://www.education-world. com/a_curr/strategy/strategy012.shtml.

Jensen, E., & Johnson, G. (1994). *The learning brain*. San Diego, CA: Turning Point for Teachers.

Lee, H. (1960). *To kill a mockingbird*. New York, NY: J.P. Lippincott Company.

McCarthy, B. (1990). Using the 4MAT system to bring learning styles to schools. *Educational Leadership, 48* (2), 31–37.

National Council of Teachers of English and International Reading Association. (1996). *Standards for the English language arts*. Urbana, IL: National Council of Teachers of English (NCTE).

Novak, J. D., & Cañas A. J. (2006). *The theory underlying concept maps and how to construct them*. Technical Report IHMC CmapTools 2006-01. Retrieved August 15, 2006, from http://cmap.ihmc.us/Publications/ResearchPapers/ TheoryCmaps/TheoryUnderlyingConceptMaps.htm.

Ogle, D. M. (2000). Make it visual: A picture is worth a thousand words. In M. McLaughlin & M. Vogt (Eds.), *Creativity and innovation in content area teaching*. Norwood, MA: Christopher-Gordon.

Poe, E. A. (1983). *The tell-tale heart*. New York, NY: Bantam Classics.

Robinson, S. M., Ph.D., Haynes, D., M.S., Richman, L., M.S., & Bode, T. (n.d.). *Teacher tools: Instructional planning: Graphic organizers*. Retrieved August 16, 2006, from http://www.specialconnections.ku.edu/cgi-bin/cgiwrap/ specconn/main.php?cat=instruction&section=main.

Tate, M. L. (2003). *Worksheets don't grow dendrites: 20 instructional strategies that engage the brain*. Thousand Oaks, CA: Corwin Press.

Townsend, G. F. (Translated by). (2002). *Aesop's fables: The bat and the weasel*. Retrieved September 10, 2006, from http://www.fairytalescollection.com/Aesop_Fables/The_Bat_And_The_Weasels.htm.